The Consolidation of the Capita

CW00833074

A Socialist History of Britain

Series edited by the Northern Marxist Historians Group

Kieran Allen, *Fianna Fail and Irish Labour: from Populism to Corporatism*

John Newsinger, *Fenianism in Mid-Victorian Britain*

The Consolidation of the Capitalist State, 1800–1850

John Saville

Pluto Press

LONDON · BOULDER, COLORADO

First published 1994 by Pluto Press
345 Archway Road, London N6 5AA
and 5500 Central Avenue
Boulder, Colorado 80301, USA

British Library Cataloguing in Publication Data
A catalogue record for this book is available from the British
Library

Library of Congress Cataloging in Publication Data
Saville, John.
   The consolidation of the capitalist state, 1800–1850 / John
Saville.
      p.   cm. — (Socialist history of Britain, ISSN 1353–5021)
   Includes index.
   ISBN 0–7453–0898–8 (hbk)
   1. Great Britain—Social conditions—19th century. 2. Great
Britain—Economic conditions—19th century. 3. Great Britain—
Politics and government—19th century. 4. Great Britain—
History—19th century. I. Title. II. Series.
HN385.S268 1995
306'.0941'09034—dc20   94–32945
                                                            CIP

ISBN   0 7453 0898 8 Hardback

A Socialist History of Britain
ISSN 1353 – 5021

98   97   96   95   94
 5   4   3   2   1

Designed and produced for Pluto Press by
Chase Production Services, Chipping Norton, OX7 5QR
Typeset from author's disk by Stanford DTP Services
Printed in the EC

Contents

Preface

Socialists have always recognised capitalism as a system of productive relations that marked a historic stage in the development of the human race. There was a great leap forward in the control of the forces of nature, and for the first time in human history there emerged the technical possibilities of providing everyone in the world with freedom from starvation and an improvement in general standards of living. The economic development which occurred in the advanced capitalist societies as a result of these technical possibilities proceeded to enrich greatly a small minority of property owners and to provide the majority with either a modest improvement in living conditions or circumstances which by any definition could only be described as poverty. Severe though that poverty was in these advanced capitalisms, it was not to be compared with the appalling and harrowing privation and utter degradation which was the lot of the greater part of the world's populations.

The history of capitalism in individual countries, and on a world scale, is a history of bloody repression by the owners of property against the mass of their own people, and by the richer countries against the less advanced and poorer nations whose boundaries encompass the majority of the peoples of the world.

'Why Are the Many Poor?' was the title of the first pamphlet published in Britain by the mild-mannered Fabian Society in the spring of 1884: a question that has never lost its relevance. It is to help answer this question, which could never be answered by the Fabian Society or by the Labour socialists of the twentieth- century Labour Party, that this present series, A Socialist History of Britain, has been inaugurated, since it is only through an understanding of the historical evolution and development of capitalist society that our present problems can be fully appreciated.

This first title in the series concerns the ways in which Britain, the first country to effect the transition to an industrial society of the modern capitalist kind, moved forward from the end of the eighteenth century to begin to solve certain of the major problems of an advancing capitalist economy. To achieve the conditions for economic and political growth there were, in the first instance, two central requirements: one was the accumulation of capital and the second was the creation of a labour force 'adapted' to the requirements of the new industrialism. The economic background is provided in Chapter 1. In Chapter 2 there develops a discussion, entitled 'The Disciplining of Labour' of the ways in which a suitably regimented labouring class was brought under the control of the owners of capital. It is an analysis that is largely absent from orthodox history texts. This chapter, which relates to a central problem of capitalist development, is followed by an examination of the emergence of the business groups, and of their ideas, who were to carry through the managerial processes of change, buying the labour-power whereby their profits were generated.

The chapter which follows is of particular importance in the political history of Britain. Britain was an old country of commercial enterprise with a well-established and powerful class of landed interests who controlled and dominated the institutions of power; there were, inevitably, political problems of crucial significance with the emergence of the new class of merchants, bankers and industrialists whose own wealth was growing fast. It was this middle class of property owners, now integrally involved with the development of industrial capitalism, who were demanding changes in economic and social policies that could only come about with at least some share of political power. Chapter 4 is concerned with the history of the ways in which the traditional ruling class of landowners began to accept the need for this sharing of power – albeit very reluctantly – and of the meaning and impact of the passing of the Reform Act of 1832 and the Municipal Corporations Act of 1835: changes that helped to complete the remodelling of economic polices which the commercial and industrial groups saw as necessary for their own future expansion.

This leaves the working people, who in the first half of the nineteenth century developed ideas and political movements that challenged their exploitation by the owners of property. The state, controlled by these owners of property at national and local level, had to evolve methods of coercion, as well as subtler ways of social control, that would curb and constrain the threats that were now coming from below. Chapter 5 deals with this. Chapter 6 discusses the climax in this confrontation between the coercive powers of the state and the great popular movement of Chartism that occurred between the years 1838 and 1848. It was in this last year that repression triumphed, leaving the decades which followed to evolve and sustain craftier and more sophisticated methods of social control.

The defeat of Chartism in 1848 meant that by the time of the Great Exhibition of 1851 the consolidation of the modern capitalist state was now in place. Changes were still to come between the different factions of property, but there was no serious conflict. The institutional structure of the state could continue to adapt itself to the increasing complexities of industrial capitalism in Britain, within a world that was itself in rapid change.

Introduction

The term 'capitalism' is often missing from the writings of many historians, and this refusal to acknowledge a determinate economic system has itself a long history. The descriptive word 'capitalism' is not to be found in the writings of Alfred Marshall or in the original Palgrave's *Dictionary of Political Economy* (1894–9), and it is missing from the index to the first (1926) volume of Britain's most liberally minded conservative historian, John Clapham. The late T.S. Ashton observed in the preface to a volume on the eighteenth century, published in 1955, that no word ending in 'ism' would be found in the pages that followed. This was a particularly foolish remark from the man who succeeded R.H. Tawney in the chair of economic history at the London School of Economics, because Tawney had already commented in somewhat tart terms on the attitudes that Ashton was to adopt. In the preface to the 1937 edition of *Religion and the Rise of Capitalism* Tawney wrote:

> When this book first appeared, it was possible for a friendly reviewer, writing in a serious journal, to deprecate in all gravity the employment of the term 'Capitalism' in an historical work, as a political catch-word, betraying a sinister intention on the part of the misguided author. A solecism of the kind would not, it is probable, occur so readily today. Obviously, the word 'Capitalism', like 'Feudalism' and 'Mercantilism', is open to misuse. Obviously, the time has now come when it is more important to determine the different species of Capitalism, and the successive phases of its growth, than to continue to labour the existence of the genus. But, after more than half a century of work on the subject by scholars of half a dozen different nationalities and of every variety of political opinion, to deny that the phenomenon exists; or to suggest that, if it does exist, it is unique among human institutions, in having, like Melchizedek, existed from eternity; or to imply that, if it had a history, propriety forbids that history to be disinterred, is to run wilfully in blinkers. Verbal controversies are profitless; if an author discovers a more suitable term, by all means let him use it. He is unlikely, however, to make much of the history of Europe

1

during the last three centuries, if, in addition to eschewing the word, he ignores the fact.

Some part of the explanation for Ashton's approach must lie in the years of the Cold War. The late 1940s and most of the 1950s were years of reaction which much affected the ideas and values of intellectuals, not least those working in academic disciplines; and the same has been true of the dozen years after 1979, the period of reactionary Toryism associated with the name of Thatcher.

We have first to define what is meant by capitalism. Marx characterised it as a particular mode of production, by which he referred not merely to the conditions of technology – which he described as the state of the productive forces – but to the ways in which the means of production were owned and to the relationships between the individuals or groups in society that resulted from their connections with the processes of production. The historical emergence of capitalism as a new mode of production involved the concentration of ownership of the means of production in the hands of a small minority of the population – the capitalist class – and the presence of a large propertyless class for whom the sale of their own labour-power was the only source of their livelihood. It was particular and peculiar to the capitalist mode of production that labour-power had itself become a commodity to be bought and sold in the market like any other object of exchange. Those who sold their labour-power – children, women and men – were during most periods in the historical evolution of capitalism legally free to sell their power to work as they chose. Labour-power as a commodity has been the distinguishing feature of the capitalist mode of production compared, for example, with the feudalism that preceded many of the capitalist societies of today. The direct subordination of the worker to a capitalist is then the crucial determinant of the capitalist mode of production. But because in the case of Britain, for instance, we are referring to several centuries of change and growth, the particular shape of that subordination has changed in many ways; though not in its basic principle. In order to live we have to eat, and to the 'dull compulsion' to labour there is no alternative save for those who own property.

This is broadly the model that Marx elaborated in the final section of Volume 1 of *Capital*. He used Britain to illustrate the evolution of capitalist society from the feudal regime of medieval times. After a preliminary chapter (Chapter 21), Marx then proceeded to discuss the ways in which the agricultural population had become separated from the land many of them owned, as a result of which there emerged a landless labouring class. Alongside them there appeared by the end of the sixteenth century a class of capitalist farmers – 'rich, considering the circumstances of the time' – who began working the land on a capitalistic basis. Over time the decline of the self-subsistence unit was paralleled by the growth of the home market for commodities. Marx emphasised the widening of the market as a crucial by-product of the structural changes in the countryside, and a necessary element of the development of industrial capital, as being part of the whole historical process of change over three centuries. He followed this discussion of the home market with an account of the origins of the industrial capitalist, although there is a more extended analysis in Volume 3 of *Capital*, published after his death. In the original chapter of Volume 1 Marx was mainly concerned with the various sources of pre-industrial wealth which could later be turned into industrial capital. He explained that the different parts of pre-industrial capital existed at the end of the seventeenth century as:

> a systematical combination, embracing the colonies, the national debt, the modern mode of taxation, and the protectionist system. These methods depend in part on brute force, e.g. the colonial system [here Marx was referring, *inter alia*, to the slave trade]. But they all employ the power of the State, the concentrated and organised force of society, to hasten, in hothouse fashion, the process of transformation of the feudal mode of production into the capitalist mode, and to shorten the transition. Force is the midwife of every old society pregnant with a new one. It is itself an economic power.

What Marx was doing in these brilliantly suggestive chapters was to outline in summary form the preconditions which were leading towards the acceleration of economic growth associated with the development of industrial capitalism. Above all, Marx understood that in British history over three centuries the relationship between the growth of a capitalistic agriculture, with its accompanying social changes, was integrally involved with the changes in industry and trade in the rest of the economy. Marx assumed in his model that sometime after the middle of the eighteenth century the basic economic framework for industrialisation was more or less completed. Naturally there was to be much unevenness in future economic and social change, and full note must be taken of the lags in as well as the advances of industrial organisation right down to the end of the nineteenth century. But around the beginning of the third quarter of the eighteenth century, with a dynamically expanding capitalist agriculture, a high rate of capital accumulation, the emergence of relevant financial techniques and institutions, an increasingly favourable market situation both at home and abroad, a developing transport infrastructure (always requiring large capital inputs), a legal system that was slowly adapting itself to the demands and necessities of the market, and, not least, the beginnings of a surge forward in the numbers of proletarianised labourers – especially in the younger age groups – the conditions for the industry state of the nineteenth century were firmly in place.

The economic organisation, or the economy, lies within the wider society or state, and it is the connections between the economy, and the politics and politicians of the state in the first half of the nineteenth century, that provide the general subject matter of the present work. The capitalist mode of production has always produced very marked inequalities in income and wealth. Ownership of the means of production normally means wealth, and wealth means power, and the concentration of wealth in Britain may be illustrated by a simple listing of figures. By 1911–13, after more than a century of industrial capitalism, one per cent of the population of Britain owned 69 per cent of all personal wealth; five per cent owned 89 per cent, and 10 per cent owned 92 per cent. That left 90 per cent of the total population sharing eight per cent of all personal wealth between them.

A theory of the state is a theory of society and for the most part this is not our main concern. It is the agencies and institutions of the British state upon which our analysis is concentrated. What, for example, was the social composition of government and what economic interests did government represent? Classical Marxism and especially Leninism assumed that the state is an institution whereby the dominant exploiting class imposes its power upon society and defends its privileges; but while this is acceptable as a first approximation, Marxist studies in the past few decades have developed a much more sophisticated and subtle analysis of state power. The writings of Antonio Gramsci have been an important catalyst in this regard; and the question of how governments in bourgeois democracies achieve popular consent is recognised as a problem of major importance and significance. Such a recognition is part of the discussion of what has become known as the 'relative autonomy' of the state, and an appreciation of the complexities of the relations between the economic and the political is a necessary part of historical analysis.

The central theme of this present work assumes that by 1850 most of the obstacles in the way of the capitalist class making money had been removed, and that the industrial economy was operating in a smoother and more efficient way than it had been 50 years earlier. The state of the harvests, after the first quarter of the nineteenth century, no longer exercised the lumpy effects upon the rest of the economy as had been the case in the eighteenth century. Fluctuations within the economy now arose from movements internal to the state of trade and industry. There were still economic crises of course, and still many failures of business and financial institutions, but in Britain after 1850 the flow of business generally was less erratic than it had been earlier.

There were two political problems of central importance for the business classes in the first half of the nineteenth century. One was the question of power-sharing with the traditional ruling groups of the landed aristocracy. For reasons we shall consider later, there was no possibility of anything approaching a total displacement of political power. Instead there had to be a sharing of power, at the centre and at the local and regional levels; at the same time, the commercial and industrial bourgeoisie could not contemplate any government which consistently operated economic policies contrary to the central interests of the capitalist classes. In practice, in spite of the frenzy which overtook so many parliamentary occasions – as in the years of the debates over the repeal of the Corn Laws – the acceptance of the business demands during the 1830s and 1840s proved less traumatic than many contemporaries tended to believe possible. Laissez-faire and free trade soon became articles of faith for most politicians; when the dramatic fall in agricultural prices occurred from the mid-1870s onwards – affecting especially the arable areas – no one seriously contemplated the return of protectionism for the agricultural interest.

The second political problem of these first decades of the nineteenth century, culminating in the great Chartist movement, was the threat to all property from below: from the labouring people. Until this serious threat of physical force was curbed and contained there would always remain uncertainties and anxieties. Again, there was never the possibility of reaching any complete solution. The capitalist order generated conflict as part of its normal operating methods, but it was necessary to find ways of disciplining the workforce within the workplace – developing the processes of adaptation – and then, in the wider political context, of encouraging a social consciousness which began to accept existing society as natural and legitimate. In these respects 1848 was the decisive year, with the imprisonment of Chartism's militant leadership and many of its second-line activists. It was not until the revival of socialism 30 years later that there was an alternative to existing society which commanded the support of even small minorities of the working people. After 1848 we have the extraordinary historical spectacle of the most proletarian country in the industrial world being without an independent working-class political party until the early years of the following century.

CHAPTER 1

The Economic Background

The Civil War and the Interregnum of the middle decades of the seventeenth century eliminated for ever the absolutist role of the monarchy in Britain. As the French Ambassador explained to his King after the Restoration: 'This government has a monarchical appearance, and there is a King, but it is far from being a monarchy.' In the last resort, Parliament now had control over the finances of the country, and the subsequent events which removed James II from the throne in 1688 confirmed the fundamental alignment between the aristocratic landlords and politicians, and the mercantile bourgeoisie. These political changes of 1660 and 1688 marked the beginning of Britain's new position among the major powers of Europe – the result of internal economic development, an acceleration of overseas trade and the first stages of the long period of wars against commercial competitors. The last 40 years of the century saw in particular a marked expansion of foreign trade. In 1640 some 80–90 per cent of exports from London were of woollen cloth; and London was by far the most important port in Britain. By the end of the century imports had increased by about a third and exports by somewhat more than half, the increase being almost entirely due to the growth of a re-export trade in commodities from North America, the Caribbean and the Far East.

This expansion of overseas trade continued throughout the eighteenth century at a rate of growth higher than the general increase in the domestic economy; and there were significant changes in its geographical distribution. On the export side, Europe in 1700 had taken about four-fifths of British-produced goods and an equally high proportion of re-exports; by the end of the century the former North American colonies were the most important single region for British exports, followed by the Caribbean, with Europe accounting for less than a quarter. It was the markets of the American mainland, whose population grew from 300,000 in 1700 to three million in 1776, that provided the most spectacular openings for British domestic goods. The reasons were obvious. It was a frontier society, but behind the frontier there was emerging a smaller yet growing version of the British home market. Most of the demand from what was a prosperous rural society was for goods already produced for the home market in Britain: textiles,

6

household furnishings of all kinds, construction tools, agricultural implements, and the many other iron (and some steel) goods that the rapidly growing metal centres of Birmingham and Sheffield were producing in ever-increasing quantities.

A lively sector of a developing economy inevitably encourages the general pace of change, and the economic impact of a successful commercialising agriculture upon other areas of trade and industry was considerable. By the last quarter of the eighteenth century there was in place a tripartite social structure in the countryside: that of landlord, capitalist tenant-farmer and wage-labourer. There were striking differences from the position in the rest of Europe: Britain saw the virtual elimination of the peasantry, the growth of the large farm – large certainly when compared with most of western Europe – and the remarkable concentration of landholding by the aristocracy and the gentry. The products of agriculture were important for various manufacturing sectors as well as for the food markets: wool for the textile industries; wheat for the corn-millers, distillers, starch-makers and as flour for use by bookbinders, linen printers and paper-hangers; barley for the maltsters; the hides of cattle and their fat for the tanners; sheep hides and fat for the soap-boilers and candlemakers. The list could be much extended.

The growth of international trade encouraged all varieties of manufacturing production and the enlargement of ports and their facilities, and a quickening of coasting trade. This expansion of overseas trade also stimulated the demand for an enlargement of financial mechanisms and institutions which could provide credit for many purposes; these included marine insurance. The hazards of war at sea were especially troublesome. Between 1688 and the Battle of Waterloo Britain was at war, on land or sea and usually both, for about 70 years out of a total of 127 years. War in its many aspects is a costly business. In the years between 1689 and 1697 some 74 per cent of total government expenditure was for military purposes, and for the rest of the eighteenth century the proportion was never below 60 per cent. These figures were not out of line with the military expenditure of other European states, although the British outlays represented a smaller part of the national income than was the case elsewhere in Europe, and economic growth continued to diminish the proportion, with the qualification that taxation always remained high.

The aim and purpose of war was to increase national power. By the end of the seventeenth century Britain was already becoming a major power in Europe, certainly a position not occupied before 1640. With the ending of the Seven Years' War in 1763 Britain not only controlled large areas and regions beyond its own shores, but effectively controlled the main sea highways. We have, in short, a transformation of Britain into a major power within two or three generations – the result in John Brewer's words, of the creation of a 'fiscal-military' state of remarkable efficiency and effectiveness.

The most important fiscal responsibility, then, of the English state after 1688 was the collection of the vast sums required to finance the rapidly growing costs of war. This problem continued throughout the eighteenth century. British governments in their search for increased revenues were for the most part limited to voluntary loans and the levying of taxes. There were other options available which some European states used as much as they could – the selling of honours or public offices, or the debasement of the coinage – but these were not acceptable, in the main, to eighteenth-century England. Loans required the confidence of the investing public, and that confidence would only be forthcoming if the general condition of the state's finances was deemed to be capable of ensuring that regular payments of interest would always be made. Governments must have a regular income, and a regular income could only be secured by a tax system which met two basic requirements: first, that the level of taxation was sufficiently high to meet the financial needs of the state; second, and much more difficult to achieve in the Europe of the eighteenth century, that taxation should be efficiently and effectively collected. In the case of the English state after 1688 both these requirements were fulfilled. During the eighteenth century taxes increased to higher levels than those of any country in Europe, but the greatest achievement of the century was their effective collection.

There were three main groups of taxes: the land tax, custom duties on goods imported, and the excise taxes on home-produced commodities. The land tax, as its name suggests, fell most heavily upon the landed classes, and down to about 1715 provided the greater part of the revenue raised by the three groups noted above. The contribution of the land tax, however, declined quite sharply from the third decade onwards, and as the eighteenth century progressed indirect taxation came to be the chief source of the total tax revenue. The returns from customs naturally grew steadily, although large-scale smuggling reduced the amounts that could potentially have been collected. It was the excise receipts that became the bedrock of the revenue system. Excise taxes were levied on a fairly limited number of commodities, the most important being beer, cider, malt, hops, wines and spirits, leather, soap, starch, candles and silk. These were all commodities whose sales in an expanding economy could be expected to grow steadily. With the exception of wines, spirits and raw silk, they were all products of, or were derived from, the output of domestic agriculture; and with the commercialisation of agricultural operations, which included rising productivity, an increasing output could normally be relied upon, in spite of the fluctuations in climate and weather conditions.

Here the efficiency of tax collection must again be emphasised. The organisation of the Excise Office was the most impressive administrative development of the eighteenth century. It was the biggest of all government departments, the one which had most direct contact with ordinary people. Moreover, the relative absence of corruption from the Office was remarkable by European standards.

Together with this general increase in taxation, the state also embarked upon large-scale borrowing. The foundation of the Bank of England in 1694 produced the formal creation of the National Debt, and it was around the state's continued borrowing that there emerged a range of financial institutions involved in the buying and selling of government stocks, the underwriting of government issues, and the provision of credit for a variety of government enterprises, mainly overseas.

The Bank of England was given a monopoly of joint-stock banking in England (but not in Scotland) and by the middle of the eighteenth century it had become the lender in the last resort to the London financial community. The Bank managed government business, issued its own notes (which were increasingly accepted as legal tender) and practised as a banker in its own right. The second part of the banking structure that emerged at this time comprised the London bankers, whose origins went back to Restoration England. During the course of the eighteenth century there developed an important divergence in the specialisations of the banks of the West End – which were often among the earliest established – and those in the City of London. The West End banks had little to do with mercantile activity but were mainly concerned with the financial resources of the rich: matters of loans, mortgages and investment in government stocks. The City banks, by contrast, were intimately connected with the growth in trade and industry, with the discounting of bills of exchange, and with making short-term loans to stockbrokers and financial dealers in general. During the closing decades of the eighteenth century the number of City banks grew rapidly. In total there were around 30 in London at the mid-century and about 50 in 1770. Then came a much more rapid increase, with new and important relations being established with banks outside London which were known as country banks, whether they were to be found in towns or in country areas. There developed a discount market whereby the new group of discount brokers discounted bills of exchange from the industrial and commercial areas outside London, using the surpluses from the agrarian regions for their longer term settlement. The London discount market became an essential link in the circulation of capital resources by which agricultural wealth, broadly defined, assisted in the general financing of trade and manufacturing. Thomas Richardson, a Quaker who had worked in London as agent for the Gurneys of Norwich, became the leading bill-broker in these early years. At the end of the Napoleonic Wars his turnover in bills was more than £13 million; by 1823 it was £20 million.

The transition to the industrial state, it must be emphasised, was never smooth and even. On the contrary, it was turbulent, disorderly and in social and political terms often violent. In a society which still produced the greater part of its own food supply, the success or failure of the harvest would always have an impact upon the economy as a whole. The demand for food, especially bread, was notably inelastic. A poor harvest would immediately increase prices and the consequences of a reduction in consumers' expenditure in other sectors of the market would be quickly transmitted. The cyclical movements of the economy in the eighteenth century could inflict great hardships upon the labouring masses. Moreover, any decline into economic depression, which could be quite sudden, would result in widespread failures of businesses and financial institutions, many of which were narrowly based. The banking system outside London, for example, was subject to the repeated collapse of individual establishments. In part this was due to technical inexperience, in part to the fact that provincial banks were often not organised on a branch basis, in part to the quite violent and sudden movements within the economy. The contemporary Scottish system encouraged branch banking, and the constant failures south of the border made the English appreciate the advantages that a more broadly based system would offer. But as late as 1825, a year of severe crisis, no less than 80 country banks were forced to close their doors; even one well-established London bank, which acted as agent for 43 banks in the provinces, also failed.

What was usually termed the Industrial Revolution – located roughly between the last quarter of the eighteenth century and the 1830s – has become a somewhat unfashionable description, to the point where it is either no longer used or its meaning denied. Emphasis in orthodox texts is now upon the relative slowness of economic growth in the period of the Industrial Revolution and upon rates of growth that were higher in the earlier decades of the eighteenth century than used to be supposed. There is also more stress upon the marked unevenness of technological change between different industries and between different regions. The persistence of traditional methods of working well into the nineteenth century has been greeted by some historians – especially social historians – as a discovery of seminal importance: a 'discovery' documented in detail by John Clapham in 1926 in the first volume of his economic history of modern Britain. He began his summary statement in Chapter 5 thus: 'Because no single British industry had passed through a complete technical revolution before 1830, the country abounded in ancient types of industrial organisation and in transitional types of every variety.'

The technical components of the first stage of modern industrialisation in Britain were coal and iron. Already by 1700 Britain was producing nearly 3 million tons of coal a year. More than half of this went for domestic uses; the rest for a variety of industries which included ironworking, brewing and lime-burning. The exhaustion of charcoal supplies was already forcing industries to relocate themselves to meet their fuel requirements and to experiment with coal as an alternative. The first coking process was used in the Coalbrookdale ironworks in 1709, although it took another half century before coke began to be used by other ironmasters. Experimentation with the production of good-quality bar iron was not successful until the 1780s, when two inventions by Henry Cort solved the problem. In 1784 patents were taken out by Henry Cort and also Peter Onions for a new version of the puddling process in the production of bar iron, and Cort combined with his puddling process improved rolling machinery. The combination of puddling with the new rolling processes saved both time and fuel and produced superior quality bar iron. By this time James Watt's steam engine was already working satisfactorily, with John Wilkinson's cylinders providing the accuracy in boring that was required, and with Boulton's business acumen ensuring the financial stability of the enterprise. By 1800 there were about 500 of the Watt–Boulton engines in operation.

With coal, efficient varieties of iron and the new source of energy which replaced the centuries-old dependence upon local wind and water, the material bases for the industry state were now in place; in a very uneven way the new technology gradually – occasionally very quickly – began to replace traditional techniques. One direct result was the birth of some new industries, of which mechanical engineering was among the most important. The early machines had been handmade, and it was only after the end of the French wars that machinery began to be made by machinery. Maudsley's slide-rest, Nasmyth's steamhammer, planing machines and wheel-cutting engines were among the most striking inventions which created and then transformed the engineering industry. The iron age had begun.

The textile sector of the economy grew at the fastest rate from the closing decades of the eighteenth century and for most of the next half century. There were important technical developments in the cotton industry – by far the most advanced and the fastest growing of all the textile industries – but the general technology of cotton manufacture was basically quite simple. The cotton industry would certainly have grown without steam power, but having adopted the steam engine it grew more rapidly, although as late as 1840 about one-quarter of its power was still supplied by the waterwheel. Cotton was above all an export industry, relying upon the monopoly of the markets of Britain's colonial empire and also upon the opening up of the undeveloped countries of the world. At the end of our period, in 1850, textiles of all kinds made up 60 per cent by value of all UK exports, and of this total cotton yarn and fabrics accounted for about two-thirds. Even in 1870 textiles still represented some 55 per cent of all export values. The remarkable expansion of the British cotton industry – representing the most modern factory production in the first half of the nineteenth century – had the paradoxical result of sustaining and extending one of the most primitive and certainly degrading forms of economic exploitation in the modern 'advanced' world: the slave economy of the American South.

The first half of the nineteenth century witnessed a coming together of a more integrated system of industry, trade and finance. The processes of change were still uneven and lopsided; much of the traditional remained at the mid-century, but economic organisation was now moving towards a more cohesive order. The appropriate institutions were adapting, with various degrees of consonance, to the requirements of industrial capitalism. When the railway age began in 1830 with the opening of the Manchester to Liverpool line, the pace of integration quickened, with the new iron roads bringing every part of the country into closer touch with each other. At the mid-century coal production was around 60 million tons. It is probable that Britain accounted for about 20 per cent of world trade, and 40 per cent – perhaps more – of trade in manufactured goods. Even in 1870, when other nations were beginning to experience significant economic growth, it is estimated that Britain may have had about one-third of the world's manufacturing capacity.

If we look at the nineteenth century as a whole, total manufacturing production increased by 15 times between the beginning and the end of the century. The major constituents were the staple industries of coal, textiles, iron and steel and various sectors of engineering – shipbuilding, prime movers, machine tools and railway materials and railway machines of all kinds. These staple industries dominated the economy at the beginning of the twentieth century, with the groups noted above accounting for around 40 per cent of all output, three-quarters of all exports and a quarter of all employment. The proportion of agriculture, forestry and fishing in gross national income by industrial distribution was 32 per cent in 1801. It was by far the largest sector of the economy, although by 1851 the proportion was 20 per cent and by 1901 it was down to six per cent. The population of Britain – Ireland being omitted – was 10.7 million at the time of the first census in 1801; it was 37 million in 1901. With this extraordinary growth in population went an equally remarkable shift from the country to the towns. The ratio of urban to rural inhabitants stood at 20:80 in 1801, at about 50:50 at mid-century and at 80:20 in 1901. The number employed in all agricultural work was 1.3 million at the beginning of the twentieth century, with over seven million workers in total in transport and communications, coal and quarrying, metal manufactures of all kinds, building and construction, textiles and clothing. For these last two groups female workers were also included in the figures. This was indeed the industry state.

CHAPTER 2

The Disciplining of Labour

The central problem for capitalist society in respect of its labour force was the conversion of labour, as an individual and collective unit, into an efficient and disciplined factor of production: one that would respond to the technical requirements of the system, and also to the material incentives which in the medium and long run it would be able to offer. In Britain these processes of adaptation were to be spread over several centuries; it was, in Marx's words, a matter of 'bloody discipline', a long historical evolution that coerced the mass of the labouring people into the wage-labourers of modern industrial society.

The organisation of work in the centuries before the factory became the symbol of a new industrial order produced flows of output that were uneven and irregular. The rhythm of the productive process was regulated not so much by time as by the nature and character of the work to be done; that is to say, by what is called task-work. Agricultural operations were obviously dependent upon the season and the weather within a particular season, but in other sectors of the economy before the factory age, however much market forces had entered into daily life, precise clock time was rarely a strictly controlling factor. In the outwork industries, where it was not possible to control entry to or exit from work, the labourer had a degree of management over the rate at which he or she worked, or over the amount produced in any one day. Obviously such control varied between occupations. We must also distinguish between skilled and unskilled labour, or between labour which had some leverage over the work situation and those without any such advantage.

Skilled labourers not only received remuneration at a higher level than did the unskilled, but, perhaps even more important, the regularity of their work was almost always to be contrasted with the casual nature of employment available to those without some degree of skill. It was the irregularity of work as well as low wages which caused so much poverty among the unskilled groups. This is not to suggest that skilled workers enjoyed full employment throughout their lives. They were subject, as was the whole of the labour force, to fluctuations in the trade cycle throughout the eighteenth century and subsequently. Economic and social crises were often the product of harvest failures in the eighteenth century, and the aftermath of war usually brought a downturn in economic activity; but the skilled workers, then and later, never experienced the desperate struggle for work, or the lifelong deprivation, of unskilled labourers and their families. That has been true throughout the long history of the capitalist order.

An exclusively money wage for work completed was far from universal, and the failure to pay wages at regular intervals was common. In the large dockyards belonging to government, and in other enterprises, the delay in money payments had led to the acceptance of perquisites being built into ordinary working practice. The eighteenth century accepted as normal the practice in many trades whereby workers were permitted to retain for their own consumption, or for sale in the open market, certain of the waste materials of their daily work. Thus in the dockyards shipwrights became entitled to 'chips', that is waste timber; ropes, sail canvas and cordage were some of the extras taken by other dockyard workers. Tailors gathered to themselves 'cabbage' (waste cloth); weavers, in some districts, were permitted to keep the cut ends when a piece of cloth was removed from the loom. In time these perquisites were understood as legitimate rights which belonged to the occupations in question; and the economic dynamism which encouraged specialisation offered additional possibilities for workers to establish new positions within the hierarchy of the labour process. Time hardened these customs and it was the tenacity with which the craftsmen, and others, held on to their traditional work patterns that created many problems in the transition to the factory system. The strength of convention and accepted routine found expression in many ways, and working people were fully conscious of what they would be subject to in the new factory enterprises. Thus the craftsmen of Saddleworth in Yorkshire insisted in evidence to an 1806 Committee on Woollen Manufactures:

> that the domestic system is highly favourable to the cultivation of paternal, filial and fraternal affections, the sources of domestic happiness, and the generation of good moral and civil habits, the sources of public tranquillity; that the factory system tends to the prevention of these affections and habits, and leads youth sooner into the stronger temptations

These were the words – exaggerated for many who worked under the outwork system – of craftsmen who organised their leisure as well as some patterns of their working life. Saint Monday is probably the best known of the type of 'play' within a working week. Saint Monday was the practice whereby skilled workers – the practitioners were mostly the better paid – elected to take Mondays as a day free from work. It was a tradition that lasted much longer into the nineteenth century in certain towns and particular occupations than is often recognised. In Birmingham, one of the main centres of small workshops, there were still complaints about the Monday observance in the decades after 1850. In Sheffield, another centre of metal-working artisans, an employer in the 1860s noted that in spite of his considerable control over the processes of production he still could not get his grinders to work on Tuesdays. The mass of ordinary labourers, living in varying degrees of deprivation, were always in a weak position in respect of any of their employers' demands, but feast days and festivals, often linked with the agri-cultural calendar, were enjoyed with traditional recreations such as football, cockfighting, boxing contests and bearbaiting. Marts and fairs were family occasions. All these recreational activities came out of a plebeian culture that had been evolving over the centuries.

The adaptation of the labouring masses to the requirements of the factory system was not, therefore, a straightforward or an easy historical process. In the pre-factory era it was found necessary to control labour in ways that could later be discarded once the discipline of the factory had been accepted. In every type of class society there has always been some form of compulsion to ensure that the maximum surplus can be extracted from these who provide the labour-power. In the domestic, putting-out system of eighteenth-century England, where direct supervision was not possible, fines and deductions were commonly used for work that was deemed below standard. Accessories necessary for the work process – candles, for example – were paid for by the workers themselves. Many occupations had a degree of direct compulsion. Colliers and saltworkers in Scotland had imposed upon them a second serfdom. In 1606 there was passed a statute which refused miners and saltworkers the right to seek a new master without the consent of the current employer; and there were penalties listed to be imposed upon the labourers and their new masters. By the end of the seventeenth century nearly every miner found himself, and his wife and children, bound for life to one employer. An Act of 1775 began its preamble:

> Whereas by the statute law of Scotland, as explained by the judges of law there, many colliers and coal-bearers, and salters, are in a state of bondage and slavery, bound to the collieries or salt works where they work, for life, and are transferable with the collieries and salt works ...

The 'coal-bearers' were the wives and daughters of the colliers who went down the pits to collect the coal and then carried it up on ladders to the surface. As a rule the coal-bearers were not paid a wage. This legal abasement was matched by the social degrada-tion of the mining communities in Scotland, where the colliers and their families were looked upon by the rest of the working population as approaching the subhuman. The legal bondage was only partly ended by the Act of 1775. Serfdom was not formally abolished until 1799, but before that it had been dying away rapidly. The growing demand for coal as the eighteenth century progressed required ever-increasing numbers of miners, and only improved wages would attract new entrants. By the last quarter of the century Scottish wages were higher than in the long-established mining communities of Durham and Northumberland, and a 'free' labour market had now come into being.

Miners in Scotland were exceptional in the degree of their unfreedom, but there were different grades of coercion in other mining areas as well as in other occupations. Children, and above all pauper children, were always the most easily exploited. Under laws that went back to Elizabethan times, pauper children could be apprenticed at the age of seven and not released from the apprenticeship until they were 21. They were employed in coalmines, both boys and girls, and their formal prohibition lasted until an Act of 1842, but other trades also used them. It was the large-scale employment of pauper children in the factories of the textile regions, especially Lancashire, that marked a new phase in the history of child employment. The cotton mills, located in their early years outside towns where water-power was available, exploited their child labour in such appalling ways that contemporaries, even some cotton-masters, were moved to support the first Factory Act of 1802 which applied only to pauper children. With the increasing adoption of the steam engine the mills moved into the towns, where large numbers of 'free' children were available at the factory gates.

The growth of population, and continued proletarianisation, meant that there was theoretically no labour shortage for any period of time in any major region of Britain. The reality was often different. Forty per cent of the total population of Britain at the beginning of the nineteenth century were under 15 years of age; it was their numbers as well as their cheapness, together with the fact that they could be more easily disciplined than adult workers, that accounted for the widespread employment of children in all types of industrial organisation.

There were always problems with all grades of labour, and the techniques of management moved very slowly away from coercion of various kinds to some measure of incentive. The factory was an institution for disciplining workers, individually and collectively, into habits of regular production which maximised their output, and therefore the volume of profits. In domestic industry the hours were long, there was gross overcrowding in most rural areas, the air in the working room was foul, sickness was common and payment for work completed was often withheld; but once outside the cottage or workshop the air was clean, the water not usually polluted and there was often a patch of cultivable land. J.L. and Barbara Hammond documented the change:

> to all the evils from which the domestic worker had suffered, the Industrial Revolution added discipline, and the discipline of a power driven by a competition that seemed as inhuman as the machines that thundered in factory and shed. The workman was summoned by the factory bell; his daily life was arranged by factory hours; he worked under an overseer imposing a method and precision for which the overseer in turn had to answer to some higher authority; if he broke one of a long series of minute regulations he was fined, and behind all this scheme of supervision and control there loomed the great impersonal system.

As the Hammonds summed up the new regime: 'The machinery never tired.' Hours of work in the mills usually ran from 6 am to 6 pm. The Hammonds mostly referred to the adult male worker, but the gender and age structure of the cotton factories embraced all groups. An official enquiry in 1833 calculated that cotton mills employed 60,000 adult males, 65,000 adult females, 43,000 boys under the age of 18 and 41,000 girls under 18. About half of those in the last two groups were less than 14 years old.

It was never easy to discipline these early factory workers, even though the alternative to the factory was often starvation. Absenteeism from any one factory was high and the turnover in the early enterprises was considerable. The economic compulsion to labour, in spite of the hatred the new factories induced, was irresistible. Slowly but inexorably the domestic system was being undermined by superior competitiveness and a factory proletariat was being formed, trained to accept the clock as the determinant of labouring hours, working to the rhythm of the machine and sluggishly adapting to the meagre incentives that began to be offered: piece-work, bonus systems and, occasionally, promotion.

In mercantilist times the emphasis had been upon coercion by poverty, the belief that raising wages above a certain minimum level would only encourage idleness. By contrast, the classical economists of the decades after 1800 argued that factory discipline itself instilled into the workforce the virtues of regularity and reliability, and that different types of remuneration would encourage a more sustained response: an early recognition of the prerequisites of the modern factory proletariat.

There were other ways of ensuring that working people laboured according to the dictates of their employers. Of those that lay outside the immediate employment situation, the law was the most compulsive and the most easily available, since the majority of cases

could be heard before local magistrates. With the decline in feudal
relationships in England there began to appear on the statute book
Acts which gave sanction to employers to compel some categories
of labourer to work. As early as the mid-fourteenth century the so-
called First Statute of Labourers provided an explicit statement:

> That every man and woman in England, free or bond, able in
> body and within three years not exercising a craft nor having
> his own wherein to live, nor land to till, nor serving any others,
> should be bound to serve such persons as should require him
> at the wages heretofore accustomed to be given.

Two centuries later a comprehensive Statute of Labourers (5 Eliz.
c.4) in 1563 repealed many of the Acts regulating wages and labour
generally which had come into being since the fourteenth century.
It now provided for the fixing of wages by local Justices of the Peace,
who could also determine hours of work and exact stringent
penalties against labourers who left their work without a permit.
Additionally, the Act prohibited any labourer from exercising a craft
until a seven-year apprenticeship had been served, but it also
required employers to hire only a fixed number of apprentices in
proportion to the total number of journeymen employed.

These laws had a varied impact, and over time they gradually
fell into disuse as the growth of the economy secured a free market
more suited to the requirements of the employing classes. The 1563
statute remained on the statute book until 1814, at which time its
repeal was vigorously opposed by craftsmen's unions and groups,
who wanted employers to continue to adhere especially to the
clauses concerning the limitation of apprentices. It was of course
much too late for this, with the tide of propertied opinion running
strongly against restrictions of any kind. Adam Smith had made
the strongest objections to the provision controlling the number
of apprentices, and by the early nineteenth century a belief in
market forces was an integral part of the ideology of the commercial
and business classes.

Combinations of workmen in defence of their working practices,
wages and general conditions of employment had become a common
feature during the eighteenth century. Mostly, although not entirely,
the members of such combinations were drawn from the ranks of
craftsmen, and these groups were to be found in a wide variety of
trades and occupations. Organisation was by no means continuous;
it was the specialised trade which provided the continuity. In some
occupations there is evidence of organisation at the beginning of
the eighteenth century; woollen-weaving, wool-combing and
tailoring can show even earlier organisation. Historians have
recovered evidence of several hundred industrial disputes during
the eighteenth century, and no doubt there are more to be identified.

The response of the employing classes – the masters against their servants – was to adapt the 1563 Act to the conditions of the eighteenth century. Some Acts were passed which specifically identified individual trades – for instance, Acts against tailors in 1721, hatters in 1777 and papermakers in 1794. At the end of the century came the general Combination Acts, as a result of which combinations of all trades were made illegal. The extent to which the Acts of 1799–1800 were applied during the next quarter of a century is still a matter of dispute, but it may be agreed that their impact and operation were patchy. Where the Acts were applied, as for example to put down strikes in the new industrial areas of the north, their effects were repressive.

Charges to Grand Juries offer pertinent insights into the minds of the propertied classes in the matter of their political and social understanding, and the quotation which follows sums up the general approach to the economic obligations of the labouring masses. These are the words of a professional judge in 1763:

> ALL COMBINATIONS by those of a Trade to raise the Price of the Commodities, tho' done in the Shape of Contracts, or Covenants not to sell under a set Rate, are condemned by the Law, and held illegal by Lord *Holt*, in a Case, called the *Plate Button-makers Case*. By the particular Statutes of this Kingdom, as well as by the Common Law, such practices are forbid; and all Workmen and Artificers combining to advance the Wages and Rate of their Labour, or to lessen their usual Hours of Work, though under the Form of By-Laws, Rules and Orders, are equally liable to the Punishments ordained by the Law. Their Clubs or Societies for that Purpose are also held unlawful, and the Persons who knowingly harbour them in their Houses for such Purposes, are deemed Keepers of disorderly Houses. I believe, no Principle is truer in Trade, that every Commodity, and the Labour attending it, will find its own true Value: That there should be one set Rate both for one and the other, seems to me unreasonable, as well as unpracticable; as it gives no Encouragement to, nor makes any Allowance for superior Skill, Strength, Diligence and Honesty; but those, who least deserved it, would be the greatest Gainers by such a Measure.

The common law of conspiracy had now been extended to cover collective action by workers, and at the same time there evolved a clearer definition of the laws concerning the relationships between masters and servants. These also derived from the original Act of 1563. During the eighteenth century the law on these questions began to be restated. While the clauses relating to limitation of hours of work and to the fixing of wages were being discarded, one important area remained. This concerned the punishment of a servant for neglecting his or her work or for leaving employment before a 'contract' had expired. There were a number of individual Acts which applied to specific trades and these were brought together in a general Act of 1823 (4 Geo.IV. c.34). It was under this Act that many thousands of prosecutions were brought until the law was completely changed in 1875.

The Master and Servants law of 1823 was not a special case of the evolving law of contract in modern capitalist society, but rather the last stage of the penal laws in the long history of the discipline of labour. As Holdsworth, the great legal historian, summed up many decades ago: the law of master and servants 'gave to the master remedies for breach of contract absolutely different from those available in the case of any other contract'. These laws remained in operation, let it be emphasised again, until the last quarter of the nineteenth century. At the centre of the Master and Servants law was the statutory provision which treated the employer and the worker as entirely unequal. A master who could be shown to have broken his contract in respect of any worker he employed was only liable in a *civil* action, whereas a servant who broke or violated his or her contract could be summarily sentenced by a local magistrate to imprisonment and hard labour, for up to three months. Let us look more closely at the procedures involved.

There were three main forms of breach of contract by the master against his servants. These were cruelty; dismissal from employment in violation of the original contract; and failure to pay wages that were owing, or their payment in kind (truck). The first of these – cruelty – mainly applied to workers in domestic service, and in terms of the number of prosecutions involved this seemed of minor importance. Reality was, without doubt, somewhat or very different. Most actions brought under the Master and Servants Acts (some eighteenth-century Acts still remained in force, beside the general one of 1823) came out of the small-master sectors of the economy; but then, as economic and social historians insist, the factory system was proceeding in uneven ways through different industries and different sections of industry. The cotton industry, as the most advanced sector by 1850, made little use of these laws. There were some exceptions to infrequent usage in large or relatively large-scale organisations – the pottery industry was certainly one – but in the main it was employers in the building firms or in small urban enterprises, as well as those who still employed the many thousands of outworkers, who used the penalties of coercion which the Acts gave them. Inevitably, as in all matters of law, ordinary people found themselves at a considerable disadvantage. To prove that a contract of employment had been broken was naturally difficult for ordinary labourers, since it was unusual for any agreement to have been written down and local magistrates were becoming increasingly reluctant to accept traditional practices as benchmarks for their decisions. Similarly, a claim for non-payment of wages could be countered by a master citing disobedience, or neglect, on the part of the servant concerned.

It needs to be emphasised that a servant was required to accept the demands of his or her employer regardless of the unreasonableness of the order in question. An important case of 1817, much quoted, involved an agricultural labourer on an annual contract who was dismissed because he refused to work further until he had his dinner, which was always eaten at the same time in the early forenoon (having breakfasted at five in the morning). The judge, Lord Ellenborough, stated the position:

> If the plaintiff persists in refusing to obey his master's orders I think he was warranted in turning him away ... It may be hard upon the servant, but it would be extremely inconvenient if the servant were to set himself up to control his master in his domestic regulations such as the time of dinner ... The question really comes to this, whether the master or the servant is to have the supreme authority.

The labourer in this case not only lost his job, but as he had been contracted for the year he lost his year's wages too. This insistence on obedience was common throughout society. A silkweaver in 1830 worked a twelve-hour shift in a west country factory and refused on one occasion to work longer hours; for this she was dismissed, and she lost her appeal. As the judge made clear, obeying the regulations of the factory meant obeying the commands of the master. In 1864, to give a late example, three miners in Derbyshire were prosecuted under the 1823 Act for 'absenting themselves' and refusing to enter a pit that was dangerous with fire damp. They were sentenced to 14 days' hard labour.

On the masters' side, prosecutions were made easier after the passing of the 1823 Act. Now the breach of contract by those designated as servants was defined in section 3 in very broad terms. Apart from clear breach of contract – where the contract was written and signed – there was a general heading of 'neglect' and 'any other Misconduct or Misdemeanour in the execution thereof or otherwise respecting the same'. The procedure was to lodge a complaint, upon oath, with a local magistrate who would then issue a warrant of arrest. If the complaint was found justified, the Justice of the Peace was empowered to order imprisonment with hard labour for a period not exceeding three months, or alternatively a reduction of wages could be imposed, in part or in whole. After coming out of prison, a worker who had been sentenced could be required to return to the original master who had laid the complaint in order to complete the contract; any refusal could be met with a further committal.

In addition to the general working of the Master and Servants Acts there were additional penalties against outworkers, the control over whom, in matters such as timekeeping, theft of materials and completion of piece-work, had always presented difficulties. An Act of 1777, for example, restated earlier statutory provisions against failure to complete work on time, and it became an offence to neglect the working-up of materials for eight consecutive days. This particular Act applied chiefly to workers in leather, of whom shoemakers were the largest numerical category, and to workers in iron, whose numbers in the region of Birmingham and the Black Country were increasing rapidly. As late as 1843 a further and similar Act was applied which covered most of the textile industries, one more indication of the continued existence of a large number of textile workers still outside the factories.

The Master and Servants Acts continued to be used against the workforce for most of the nineteenth century, until the trade union reform legislation of 1875. In that year the Employers and Workmen Act (38 and 39 Vict. c.90) expunged all previous legislation and conceded legal equality to the servant, who now was liable only to a civil action if a contract was deemed to have been broken. Until this date, however, the number of prosecutions remained high. We have no accurate statistics for the first half of the century, but we do know from the reports of individual cases that the Acts were being widely used. The figures for the 18 years from 1858 to 1875 show an average of 10,000 prosecutions a year. It has been remarked upon already that the Master and Servants Acts were mostly but not entirely used by small masters, and the high level of prosecutions indicates once again the unevenness of change within the general industrial structure. This is further indicated by the geographical distribution of prosecutions, which were irregularly distributed throughout England and Wales. As would be expected, it was the areas of outworking and those of small workshops that attracted most cases. In Birmingham and its surrounding industrial districts Master and Servant prosecutions were twice as common as in other parts of England; and in the ten years 1858 to 1867 Staffordshire had double the prosecutions of any other county in England.

The legal system, it needs to be emphasised, showed both flexibility for the masters and almost continuous bias against the labouring classes. In the first half of the century the bias was ferocious; later, as skilled workers began to build their defences, in the form especially of trade unions, the law remained consistently hostile if now somewhat less brutal and overbearing. The case of the Tolpuddle Martyrs in 1834 will always be mentioned in history

texts, but its full implications are usually missed; certainly, the con-
scientiousness with which the representatives of the propertied
classes fabricated their indictments is commonly missed. The story
may be briefly told. The background was the agrarian unrest which
exploded in its most dramatic way in the so-called Swing riots of
1830. Friendly societies and/or trade unions were either in elementary
existence or in gentrified imagination; and by the beginning of 1834
a certain James Frampton, member of a long-established family of
country gentlemen, was becoming increasingly worried about the
emergence of the trade union threat in south-east Dorset. He cor-
responded with both the Lord Lieutenant of the county and with
Lord Melbourne, the Home Secretary. It was to the latter that
Frampton turned for advice as to the way offenders should be
proceeded against, given that the amended 1825 Act still allowed
the formation of a trade union, even though its many qualifications
made it a wholly unreliable charter for labouring men. Melbourne
put the problem to his law officers, and the indictment they
produced made no reference to the 1825 Act but relied upon the
conjunction of Acts of 1797 and 1799. The latter provided that
belonging to an unlawful combination was a misdemeanour, while
the Mutiny Act of 1797, if the charge was proved, characterised
the offence as a felony for which the penalty could be seven years'
transportation.

The Assizes opened on 14 March 1834 and the next day the
hearing began. It was the responsibility of the Grand Jury to
determine whether an indictment was valid. The Grand Jury, it
should be noted, was made up of the local gentry and in this case
included James Frampton, his son Henry and other magistrates who
had actually signed the warrant for the arrest of the Tolpuddle
labourers. The foreman was the Home Secretary's brother-in-law.
It was hardly surprising that after a wholly prejudiced speech by
the judge, Baron Williams, which centred upon the 1797 Mutiny
Act and its relevance to the present case, the Grand Jury found a
true bill. It should be added that after clarifying the legal aspects
of the case, Baron Williams had then explained his views at length
upon the evils of men combining together.

The next step was to select the jury for the trial itself. Rural juries,
where landlord influence was so powerful, could normally be relied
upon, but in this case a good deal of care was taken that unsuitable
people were not included. Jury 'packing' was common practice in
Ireland in these years, but its use in England has not been much
commented on by English historians. In the Tolpuddle case there
is no doubt about the selection procedures. We know of one
exclusion, a Mr Bridle, rejected because he was a Methodist; and
there may have been others. What we do know is that the characters
of those nominated were enquired into by the officers of the court.

The counsel for the prosecution used three statutes, skilfully interwoven, to make his case: the Acts of 1797 and 1799, together with the Seditious Meetings Act of 1817. Of the two defending counsels one was effective and the other incompetent; while the judge summed up in the same terms he had used to instruct the Grand Jury. The jury was out for its deliberations for five or for 20 minutes, according to which newspaper report can be taken as reliable, and naturally found the six men guilty. They were sentenced to the maximum penalty of seven years' transportation.

The trial of the Tolpuddle labourers was a significant travesty of justice: significant because it illustrated the degree of duplicity the propertied classes were capable of if they felt their position threatened. In 1848, as we shall see, when many really were frightened that the French revolutionary contagion would cross the Channel, every senior judge who tried Chartist prisoners exhibited the bias and prejudice of Baron Williams in the Tolpuddle case. Parliamentary statutes were always helpful in curbing and confining working people, but in extreme situations, or in situations that were thought to be extreme, the law could almost always be relied upon to defend the rights of property in the way the Mutiny Act of 1797 was invoked against six labourers of Dorset who were members of the Tolpuddle Friendly Society. The law has always been flexible. On 17 December 1932 Tom Mann, national treasurer of the National Unemployed Workers Movement, and Emrhys Llewellyn, secretary of the Movement, were arrested under a 600-year-old Act of Edward III and the Seditious Meetings Act of 1877, section 23. No charge was preferred; their arrest was 'merely' a 'preventive measure', so they were told when they appeared at Bow Street magistrates' court. Since they refused to enter into recognisances concerning their future behaviour, they were both sent to jail for two months.

The operation of parish relief was a matter which probably touched the lives of ordinary men and women more closely than any other intervention by authority: either for themselves or for their relatives. Tudor governments had become involved with vagrants and the destitute in ways which led to the evolution of a Poor Law policy, culminating in the major Act of 1601. This and previous Acts required the parish authorities to raise a rate for poor relief, to put children out as apprentices and to ensure that the poor were put to work. The network of institutions that grew up to administer poor relief comprised various types, of which the houses of correction – for vagrants, prostitutes, semi-criminals – were the earliest, most being built in the late sixteenth or seventeenth centuries. Next in time came the workhouses, of which London's was the first in 1647, with Bristol's, built in 1697, probably the best known in the provinces. These were embryo workhouse–manufactories, whose main growth occurred after an Act of 1723 which specifically advocated new forms of parish employment. Gilbert's Act of 1782 began the changes which led to the Speenhamland system being widely adopted from the mid-1790s onwards: this was the system of payment of outdoor relief to labourers whose wages, in a period of rapidly rising inflation, were insufficient to meet the needs of their families. It was a political concession in an era of turbulence that undoubtedly helped to damp down areas of discontent.

From this time on, the national cost of poor relief in England and Wales soared. At the beginning of the 1790s it had been around £2 million; in 1801 it stood at £4 million, and in the peak year of 1818 – when in the aftermath of war destitution was widespread – the cost in poor rates reached nearly £8 million. It fell throughout the 1820s and was just under £7 million in 1830–1, but by this time the clamour for a reform of the system was being vigorously expressed. The new political economists, of whom Malthus, in this particular matter, was the most influential, were wholly against the provision of poor relief. Malthus took an extreme position. We must, he wrote, 'formally disclaim the *right* of the poor to support' …:

> To this end I should propose a regulation to be made, declaring that no child born from any marriage, taking place after the expiration of a year from the date of the law, and no illegitimate child born two years from the same date, should ever be entitled to parish assistance.

Malthus, in his economic thinking, was dominated by the significance of the law of population he thought he had discovered, but in his critique of the poor laws he also stressed the impact they had on the rate of capital accumulation – a drain on the wages fund.

In social and political terms, the operation of the poor laws was a matter of quite central importance. The economists had certainly won the minds of the middle classes of merchants and manufacturers, and most landlords were well aware that high poor rates meant lower rents. In historical perspective, the more complete disciplining of the working people could not be furthered as long as the system of relief was so discouraging to 'honest' labour and so contrary to the 'beneficent' workings of the market. Three months before the Reform Bill was finally enacted in 1832, the Liberal government appointed a Royal Commission to enquire into the workings of the Poor Law and to make recommendations. There may have been more prejudiced and ill-balanced commissions in the nineteenth century, although this is a difficult matter to measure. The Commission found the answers it wanted. The central conclusion of its Report, completed in February 1834, was the emphasis upon

the demoralisation of the labouring classes as a result of indis-
criminate outdoor relief to the able-bodied. Example after example
was quoted, and the most important recommendation was that
henceforth all relief to the able-bodied poor should be given only
in a well-regulated workhouse on the principle of less eligibility –
that is, the condition of the labourer on poor relief should be less
comfortable than the lowest paid worker in employment. It was
assumed that only those who were really destitute would apply for
relief and enter the workhouse. It was further assumed, and this
was part of the supposedly inescapable logic of the free market, that
there would always be work at some rate of wages.

The second recommendation related to administration. The
Commission had uncovered a wide variety of practice under the
old regime, and in order to achieve uniformity of operation it
advocated a central authority which would issue regulations and
instructions to the local authorities who were to administer relief.
In order that the unit of administration should be viable, and not
subject to immediate local pressures, small parishes should be
grouped into unions and their management elected by the local
ratepayers. The Report was uniformly critical of the magistracy,
and the recommendation of a strong executive state agency to run
the Poor Law system was the first proposal of a typically bureau-
cratic mechanism that has become so familiar in later capitalist state
development. The ideas of Bentham were a strong influence.

In practice the New Poor Law, especially in its early years, was
never able to follow strictly the intentions of those who produced
the report of 1834. Moreover, during the first decade or so the
hostility to the New Poor Law, especially in the industrial districts
of the north, was intense, swelling the general discontent that
provided the dynamic of the Chartist movement. It did, however,
restrict the payment of state benefits to male wage-labourers. In
the medium and long term the New Poor Law of 1834 was perhaps
the most important piece of social legislation passed during the
nineteenth century. Its influence was far-reaching, both in daily
practice and in the evolution of social consciousness. It confirmed
the general belief in self-help which the middle classes preached
daily, and over time it entered at least in part into the thinking of
working people. Acceptance of parish relief became an article of
shame for many sections of the working population – to have a
pauper's funeral was an unthinkable disgrace – and in these ways
the social fear and stigma of the workhouse went some way towards
creating the ethos and ideas which industrial capitalism required
of its working force. These changes did not happen immediately
and they were never fully assimilated, especially among the lower
paid groups of the working class; but the acceptance of 'A Fair Day's
Work for a Fair Day's Pay' among skilled workers and quite large

sections of the semi-skilled, as well as certain groups of labourers, was strengthened by the existence of a harsh and punitive system of poor relief. This is not, it must be emphasised, the end of the story, for what 'A Fair Day's Work' actually meant to skilled workers depended in part upon their position within the labour process; and whether the lower income groups within the working class as a whole ever accepted the notion is a highly debatable question.

By mid-century the moulding of the working class to the require-ments of an industrialising society was already under way. The strict discipline within the growing number of factories, together with the legal and social penalties now available to employers, was slowly but steadily contributing to the general historical processes of adaptation. The final defeat of Chartism, the physical and ideo-logical destruction of an independent working-class movement, was a principal contribution to the much less turbulent decades which followed. Up until the 1840s almost all the measures directed towards control over the labour force were the penal and repressive measures that have been considered in this chapter, but long-term accommodation to the new industrial order involved a complex of social factors. The first main stage of industrialisation was already well developed and what was now needed was a working-class response to the incentives, as well as the discipline, that capitalist society was going to be able to offer, not least to offset the pos-sibility of the total alienation of the masses and the vision of an entirely new kind of society. Walter Bagehot saw the problem clearly. In the introduction to the second (1872) edition of *The English Constitution,* he warned against the political combination of the working classes – an 'evil of the first magnitude' which could only be averted by political wisdom and foresight:

> They must avoid not only every evil, but every appearance of evil; while they still have the power they must remove, not only every actual grievance, but, where it is possible, every seeming grievance too; they must willingly concede every claim they can safely concede, in order that they may not have to concede unwill-ingly some claim which would impair the safety of the country.

Or, as he put it somewhat more crudely in a later passage, on this occasion specifically with reference to the House of Lords: 'They should give large donations out of income, and by so doing they keep, as they would keep, their capital intact.'

The formation of social consciousness among working people is a complicated interplay between working life and the ways that indi-viduals and groups appraise their own position in society; the attitudes they adopt towards the propertied classes who both employ them and rule them from Westminster; the identification, rejection or partial and muddled acceptance of aspects of the ideology of their 'masters'. In this general approach to the social environment into which they were born, people of all classes will be affected by the socialising processes in particular kinds of family life; by their education (if any) and by the religious beliefs of their parents and kinship groups (if any). For working people the fact of work, and the nature of work, assume an importance that is central to their general attitudes, although it may not encourage social reflexes that are exactly the same among different occupations or regions. Miners in the communities of Durham and south Wales were united in their trade unionism but different in their politics in spite of their adherence to the same kind of Nonconformity.

Education and religion have to be carefully assessed, for their influences change over time. Before 1850, the period of our present concern, educational provision was relatively meagre and where it was provided it was almost always seen as a means of social control. Some kinds of Nonconformity were already influential within certain working-class communities – London was always an important exception – but apart from its hostility to the Anglican Church it tended to exert a conservative influence; it was only in the second half of the century that Dissent became closely identified with liberalism and in some working-class groups with a more extreme radicalism. Behind these cultural and social influences, let it not be forgotten, the coercive apparatus of the state machine was always present; and the defensive/offensive attempts by working people to improve their economic and social position would always be met with obstruction and the embedded conservatism that affected all parts of British society. In the last resort physical coercion was always available.

CHAPTER 3

Merchants, Bankers and Industrialists

The use of the term 'middle class' in ordinary language is a relatively late development. For most of the eighteenth century it had become common to refer to the 'middling people' or 'middling sorts', or even 'the industrious classes', although this last might also include the respectable artisans. The sense of class did not enter fully into public discourse until the third decade of the nineteenth century; it was the Anti-Corn Law League which was probably the most important social movement encouraging the use of the term and instilling a more general consciousness of their particular position in society. There had long been 'ranks', 'orders' and 'degrees' and these descriptions were still being used in the decades after 1850, but only by traditionalists. The delineation of the divisions within social classes was now becoming a matter of common concern, and English snobbery was taking on its unpleasant Victorian obsessions.

The merchant classes went back a long way in time; many were wealthy and there had been intermarriage with the gentry. The London merchants played a central role in the years of the Civil War and their power increased steadily as international trade grew rapidly after the Restoration. Those described as merchants encompassed different groups who engaged in different types of economic activity, including, in the eighteenth century, the growing section of merchant manufacturers who organised production through the domestic or outwork system. Alongside the general increase in economic growth a network of financial structures emerged which included the beginnings of the London banking system after 1660 and a range of financial institutions which were involved in the financing of trade at home and overseas.

The first half of the eighteenth century produced the first members of the class of industrial capitalists that later developed the industry state of the following century. Ambrose Crowley built three large ironworks not far from Newcastle-on-Tyne which by the second quarter were employing around 1,000 men in total. Crowley is remembered, and his enterprises known in detail, through the survival of the extraordinary *Book of Laws* (c. 1700), which provided in immense detail the ways in which work in his factories should be organised. But he was not alone. Sir Humphrey Mackworth, a lawyer, developed an industrial centre at Neath in the late 1690s, an example of an effective innovating period. As with Crowley, Mackworth often experienced acute labour problems which he and his managers were not always able to solve. In the second half of the eighteenth century industrial capitalists were becoming much more numerous, more conscious of themselves as a class in respect of their own self-interest, especially with regard to their workers, and very early appreciated the financial benefits of price agreements with their competitors.

These early industrial employers – the Peels, Grants, Fieldens and Gregs in cotton; the Darbys of Coalbrookdale, the Guests of Dowlais and the Crawshays of Cyfartha among the ironmasters, with John Wilkinson as their most extraordinary personality – were not men of marked inventive ability but were successful largely because of their organisational qualities and their ruthlessness. Many were coarse and rough, driven by their single-minded determination to make money. Wedgwood the potter and Boulton and Watt were personalities of wide culture and firm moral values; but they were not typical of this new, thrusting breed whose central concerns were profits and accumulation. From their early days agreements in respect of prices or the division of the market were essential parts of their industrial dynamism. In 1762 the Darbys and the Wilkinsons agreed on prices for cylinders and pipes in all markets except London; and by 1777 an association of Midland ironmasters was holding quarterly meetings in order to coordinate trade policy in matters such as prices and conditions of sale. There were combinations of one sort or another in most trades, and in the later decades of the eighteenth century trade associations included manufacturers and merchants. The General Chamber of Manufacturers, established in the penultimate decade of the century and dominated by the cotton, iron and pottery trades, was deeply divided over the Anglo-French negotiations on the move towards freer trade between the two countries; while certain of the older industries, such as silk, leather, clocks and glass, were strongly dissentient. Lobbying on behalf of one's own sectional interest became increasingly prominent as economic growth continued; what united all sections of the business community was the general hostility towards the labouring people, whose own appreciation of the divide between masters and workers grew steadily.

The long evolution of capitalism in Britain slowly but inexorably influenced and altered every aspect of daily life, public and private. The ways in which a general law of contract came to be accepted as part of business practice were part of a wider ideological transformation dating from the sixteenth century. The elements of a contract law have been situated in Tudor and early Stuart times. By then what lawyers would describe as 'executory promises' became matters which came before the courts, and damages for promises broken, resulting in profits being lost because of breaches of promise, could be upheld. 'By mid-eighteenth century', a legal historian writes, 'Contract was advancing as one of the great organising categories of liberal thought'; and while there were many aspects of modern contract law missing from Blackstone's *Commentaries* (1765–69), he recognised the growing importance of contract law for the expanding business sectors and described the basic terms of a number of different kinds of contract. There were important differences in the ways that the common law developed in the legal areas of contract compared with equity – the former representing a stark view of freedom and the sanctity of contract, the latter administered by the court of Chancery. The nineteenth century witnessed not a revolution but a flowering of the ideas that had been developing in the previous centuries, and the business community was not inexpertly served by the legal judgements that came from the Bench. It was the cumbersome and costly procedures that vegetated, and not until the second quarter of the nineteenth century did reform of the organisation and business procedures of the courts really reach the early stages of serious and sensible improvement. Brougham's famous speech of 1830 on judicial reform was part of the beginning of the processes of change, but institutions so often lag behind the ideas which have come to be accepted.

The establishment of 500 county courts in England and Wales in 1846 by the Small Debts Act of that year was perhaps the most important single, and wholly desirable, change that occurred during the first half of the century. But change, in law as well as in legal procedures, proceeded, although too slowly. It would certainly have been much helped if the senior law officers of the Crown as well as the senior members of the judiciary had not been in the habit of living so long. Nevertheless, by mid-century the essential framework for reasonably effective business practice between contracting parties was now in place. There was still much to be done. Joint-stock status had been granted to banks in 1826 and 1833, but general limited liability did not arrive until 1856, although it must be noted that there was markedly little demand for the principle before the 1850s. Bankruptcy law was to prove more difficult to settle; but in this and other areas of commercial law the reforming zeal of the second quarter of the nineteenth century had begun a process of change and adaptation which was now irreversible.

One aspect of the legal changes has become more important to economic historians in recent decades. This is the law relating to patents. The Statute of Monopolies dated from as early as 1624, as Parliament's attempt to stop James I from granting monopoly privileges in trade to his favourites or particular interest groups, but there was one clause in the Act which specifically exempted inventions that could be shown to be a 'manner of new Manufacture'; for these, patents limited to 14 years were introduced. Further, those who introduced a foreign technique into Britain and established an enterprise not previously in existence could also claim patent rights (although this particular provision, while formally remaining on the statute book, became less important as industrialisation proceeded). The introduction of the right to monopoly control for a given period as well as the formation of monopoly trading companies were part of the general commercial sentiment to advance British development in an era of intense competition from the more advanced countries of France and the Netherlands. The procedures were cumbersome and the costs high, and before the mid-eighteenth century the number of patents registered was few. For the decade 1750–9 the average number a year was nine; in 1760–9 it was 21, but by 1801–9 the average was 112. By the 1840s the annual total had risen to 458.

The insistence upon developing a commercial and industrial lead, a central theme of English mercantilist writing, was indicated by a series of parliamentary Acts, passed mainly between 1750 and 1786, which prohibited the export of tools and machinery. This was abolished only in 1841; by which time of course the British felt sufficiently confident in their general industrial superiority to accept free trade in ideas. The legal procedures in respect of patents remained ponderous and legal precedents confusing. The important change came in 1852 when a new Patent Office was established and legal costs were reduced. Patent law, however, although the practice had been simplified, remained a matter of major controversy and it was examined by a Royal Commission in 1864 and by a further Select Committee in 1872. In spite of the very considerable problems which faced the courts in the determination of patent rights and the widespread political objections to the principles involved, which many thought directly infringed the ideas of laissez-faire, the British patent system was not substantially modified until the twentieth century.

Economic thought in the later seventeenth century began to respond to the material changes in English society, although a full statement of the directions economic developments were taking was achieved only when Adam Smith published *An Inquiry into the Nature and Causes of the Wealth of Nations* in 1776. His work was both a summing up and a starting point for the classical school whose structure was completed by David Ricardo some 40 years later. In the century before Adam Smith the almost exclusive concern with value and price arising out of exchange had been shifting towards interest in production. Sir William Petty (1623–87) was not only the pioneer of economic statistics, he was also a pioneer of remarkable insight into the theoretical problems of the emerging capitalist structures. His writings include a theory of wages and of value, profit and interest, and his concentration upon labour as the source and measure of value was followed through by later political economists before Smith, of whom John Locke, Sir Dudley North and Sir James Steuart were among the most prominent. The Physiocrats in France – Turgot and Quesnay in particular – were also closely studied by Smith, although he was critical of their emphasis upon agriculture.

A substantial part of *The Wealth of Nations* was devoted to a vigorous and wide-ranging critique of what Smith called the mercantilist system. He attacked in precise terms the system of extensive government regulation, the widespread distribution of special privileges for individuals and corporate bodies, and the host of obstacles in the way of the free movement of people and goods. Smith has come down in historical understanding among the Anglo-Saxon countries as emphasising self-interest in human conduct, and as insisting that natural laws regulating economic activities should not be interfered with by the state. In popular mythology Adam Smith has been accepted as the theorist of the business community in industrial capitalism, with those interests being interpreted as the minimum of interference from governments, a free market in goods and the absence of any regulation within labour markets.

When he died in July 1790, however, Adam Smith was regarded as something of a subversive. His politics have always been difficult to determine in precise terms, but his views on the corruption of the society he lived in, his acerbic hostility to the Established Church of England, and his very low opinion of the morality of the business community were clearly set down in *The Wealth of Nations* and in the sixth and much revised *Theory of Moral Sentiments*, which was published not long before his death. Adam Smith was a liberal with radical views about the abuses of his own society. He must be read within the conditions of his times, for his advocacy of self-interest and economic freedom were for him the ways in which society would eliminate special privileges, and which would prevent those engaged in profit-making activities from operating in anti-social ways. Smith assumed, as a given fact, that those who practised commercial and business activities would always act in ways that would increase their own rewards at the expense of the rest of the community. What was needed was a society in which businessmen pursuing their own self-interest would be compelled to enhance the welfare of the whole community. Adam Smith believed, in the context of the particular period in which he lived, that the only way of curbing the natural predatory instincts by which the business community lived was through effective competition in the marketplace. He also believed that a policy of laissez-faire would mean a greater equality of opportunity, which itself would result in a greater equality of income.

In time Adam Smith would no doubt have been bowdlerised, laundered and purged of his radical, perversive ideas – a characteristic tendency of the English with regard to their dead Radicals – but his transformation into the conservative theoretician of the developing capitalist order happened within a decade of his death. Again it is the context of the times that must be examined. The revolution in France in 1789 threatened to turn the world upside down. In Britain it was the starting point for a new era of both radical activity and counter-revolution of a notably hysterical kind; and nowhere was political reaction more effectively practised than in Scotland. The famous, and infamous, sedition trials began early in 1793, sending waves of protest, and fear, throughout the country. Thomas Muir, Maurice Margarot, William Skirving and Joseph Gerrald were among those convicted of sedition and transported to Botany Bay. Their crime was the organisation of a National Convention; their most prominent judge the Lord Justice-Clerk, Lord Braxfield. Lord Cockburn, who as a child knew Braxfield, wrote this of him in his distinguished *Examination of Trials for Sedition*, written in 1853 and finally published in 1888:

> Braxfield was a profound practical lawyer, and a powerful man; coarse and illiterate; of debauched habits, and of grosser talk than suited the taste even of his gross generation; utterly devoid of judicial decorum, and though pure in the administration of civil justice where he was exposed to no temptation, with no other conception of principle in any political case except that the upholding of his party was a duty attaching to his position. Over the five weak men who sat beside him, this coarse and dexterous ruffian predominated as he chose. He had the skill to conceal his influence by making what he wished, be said or done by his brethren; but everybody who understood the scene knew whose mind was operating. *'Bring me prisoners, and I'll find you law'*, was said to be his common answer to his friends, the accusers, when he learned that they were hesitating ... Except Civil and Scotch Law, and probably two or three works of indecency, it may be doubted if he ever read a book in his life. His blamableness in these trials far exceeds that of his brethren. They were weak; he was strong. They were frightened; he was not. They followed; he, the head of the court, led.

Braxfield frightened many in the Scotland of these years, including Dugald Stewart, the most prominent academic disciple of Adam Smith and a long-serving professor of moral philosophy at the University of Edinburgh. About the same time in early 1793 as the sedition trials were being heard, Dugald Stewart read a paper to the Royal Society of Edinburgh, later published under the title *Account of the Life and Writings of Adam Smith*. Stewart cowed before the storm of reactionary opinion. He fudged Smith's radical opinions, for the real Smith, Stewart averred, was a sober public philosopher and his reputation for certain 'extreme' opinions was undeserved. It was Adam Smith the conservative theorist whom Stewart presented in his university lectures, and it happened that among the generations of students who listened to him were many who were to become important in British political life. During the French wars it became the practice of aristocratic families – those of Whig persuasion in particular – to send their sons to Edinburgh University as an alternative to the Grand Tour; and many future Whig politicians and men of letters listened to Dugald Stewart's conservative version of Adam Smith. Palmerston – who was not a Whig at this time – actually lodged with Stewart. His contemporaries included Francis Horner, Henry Brougham, Sydney Smith and Henry Petty (later Marquis of Lansdowne), most of whom were among the original founders of the *Edinburgh Review*. From Stewart they absorbed what was becoming the economic 'commonsense' of middle-class Britain. The three leading personalities of the government in 1848 – Lord John Russell, Palmerston and Lansdowne – had all been students at Edinburgh and had all heard Dugald Stewart. There were, it should be noted, other popularisers of the simplistic Adam Smith; these included Harriet Martineau, Charles Knight and the Society for the Diffusion of Useful Knowledge.

The parliamentary Reform movements of the 1780s had not involved the commercial and industrial middle classes to any notable extent, and the wars with France over more than two decades tended to damp down the sentiment for change among the middle classes. But the number of the movements was now growing. Middle-class Nonconformist groups in particular developed a shared sense of living in a society in which they were excluded from political power at national and also at local level. Moreover, there was much they increasingly disliked in this society. Unitarianism was especially important among the Nonconformist sects. Their members had a common educational background; they normally married within the group and their liberal intellectual concerns were fostered by the growing number of provincial literary and philosophical societies. Their approach was anti-authoritarian. When the anti-slavery movement was gaining prominence, it was the various groups of Dissenters who were actively involved, and appreciation of the cruelties and injustices in their own society developed apace. Their social concerns were linked with their business interests. During the last decade of war many merchants and manufacturers in the north and the Midlands felt that their economic interests were being adversely affected by government policies, and the passing of the Corn Law in 1815 confirmed the belief that the Parliament of aristocratic landowners was indifferent to the middle-class interest.

Reforming ideas began to spread more rapidly after the wars came to an end and once the immediate aftermath of war – economic depression and popular discontent – had passed. This was, as we shall discuss later, much helped by the considerable expansion of serious journalism, represented especially by the quarterly magazines which followed the founding of the *Edinburgh Review* in 1802. In the stream of ideas which flowed through the newspapers and journals of these early decades of the nineteenth century no personality was more important in terms of the stimulus he gave to new thinking on old problems than Jeremy Bentham.

Bentham was born in 1748 and his formative intellectual influences were those of the Enlightenment, which in England meant the school of Locke. Locke represented reason and free thought, and Bentham became, in the words of John Stuart Mill in his famous essay on Bentham, the 'great subversive', the critic of existing institutions and practices, the 'father of English innovation'. Until almost the end of the eighteenth century the reform of the law was Bentham's major preoccupation (he had been trained as a barrister), and his main work in politics came after he had passed the age of 50. Bentham always tended to develop his ideas to what he considered their logical conclusion; and there were times when he was right. But this is not how reform politics work in a country so encrusted with the past and so embedded with conservative traditions as was the Britain of the early nineteenth century.

The middle classes, it must be remembered, never forgot the history of revolutionary France and they were constantly reminded of the problems and the dangers of too rapid change when they listened to the ultra-radical doctrines of their own working people throughout the whole of the first half of the century. When, therefore, Bentham produced his *Plan of Parliamentary Reform* in 1817 which called for annual elections, secret voting, equal electoral districts and the enfranchisement of all adult males who were able to read, these were not parts of a reform programme which the business classes could possibly support. Sir James Mackintosh wrote a lengthy comment in the *Edinburgh Review* pointing out that universal suffrage would give a permanent majority to the labouring classes, those without property, and all other sections of society would be threatened. His tone and sentiments were exactly those of the historian Macaulay when he opposed the presentation of the Chartist national petition in the House of Commons in 1842. Civilisation, said Macaulay, rests upon the security of property, and to give the vote to those without property would be destructive of the whole of society.

It was Bentham's disciples and followers, rather than Bentham himself, who argued his ideas through the journals and all the other means of disseminating new beliefs and innovative doctrine. Between 1818 and 1824 there was published the sixth edition of the *Encyclopaedia Britannica*: virtually a Benthamite manifesto. J.R. McCulloch, representing the conservative mainstream of political economy, wrote most of its economic essays; and James Mill included his famous 'Essay on Government', later published in pamphlet form. Mill argued the case for representative government against the existing oligarchical system, but universal suffrage, he insisted, was not a necessary condition to obtain adequate and sufficient 'representation'.

The *Edinburgh Review*, the first of the great quarterlies, reflected the liveliness and vitality of late eighteenth-century Scottish society. It was Whig in its politics and general outlook at a time when some sections of Whiggism were beginning to project vigorous reforming characteristics. In its early years the *Edinburgh* was a journal of political enlightenment, of a middle-class kind, and with an invigorating crusading zeal. As Sydney Smith wrote in a famous passage many years later:

> To appreciate the value of the *Edinburgh Review*, the state of England at the period when the journal began should be had in remembrance. The Catholics were not emancipated – the Corporation and Test Acts were unrepealed – the Game Laws were horribly oppressive – Steel traps and Spring Guns were set all over the country – Prisoners tried for their lives could have no counsel – Lord Eldon and the Court of Chancery pressed heavily upon mankind – Libel was punished by the most cruel and vindictive imprisonments – the principles of Political Economy little understood – the Law of Debt and of Conspiracy were upon the worst possible footing – the enormous wickedness of the Slave Trade was tolerated – a thousand evils were in existence, which the talents of good and able men have lessened or removed; and these efforts have been not a little assisted by the honest boldness of the *Edinburgh Review*.

Sydney Smith published these words in 1839, at a time when the political situation had changed in certain striking ways since the passage of Catholic Emancipation in 1829 and the Reform Act of 1832. He was right to emphasise the disappearance of some of the more unpleasant and brutal aspects of British society in the reforming second quarter of the century; what is also interesting is what he left out of his catalogue of social and political evils. The harsh working and living conditions of so many of the labouring poor were not thought worthy of inclusion, and the 'Brutilitarianism' of the New Poor Law, as Disraeli described it, went unregarded. Nevertheless, these years did see the beginnings of a framework of bourgeois democracy. It is worth noting that the Whig journals such as the *Edinburgh* were already showing a marked decline in their reforming attitudes, above all through an unquestioned acceptance of the dogmas of political economy. The background to this was the turbulent decade of Chartism, ending in 1848, which was to push the greater part of the middle class into political agreement with the Tory aristocracy on questions of law and order, while at the same time concentrating upon the narrow and specifically middle-class demand for the abolition of the Corn Laws.

The first Tory counterweight to the *Edinburgh Review* came in 1809 with the publication of the *Quarterly Review*, a journal which included Sir Walter Scott among its founding members. The *Quarterly* is generally characterised as representing 'enlightened' Tory attitudes. Obligations, insisted the progressive Tories, always went with property ownership, at the same time as they vigorously defended the privileges of the Established Church and the landed interest. The upstart business classes were looked upon with distaste, and among some groups there developed a critique of orthodox political economy, together with varying degrees of pater-nalism. The radical liberals of this period – the followers of Bentham around James Mill and his circle – did not establish their own journal until 1824, when the *Westminster Review* appeared. In its first years the *Westminster* was militantly anti-Establishment. The tone was set in the first issue by a famous article on the *Edinburgh Review* by James Mill, which served notice of open war on the landed aris-tocracy, the Established Church, the public schools and the universities, the law, and the existing *Reviews* and their political positions. The Mill group withdrew after four years and the *Westminster*, until its amalgamation with the *London Review* in 1836, became much less lively and more orthodox in its approach to economic and social questions.

The years which followed the end of the wars with France were remarkable for the vigour and liveliness of the public prints. One list for 1826, not complete, named 27 weeklies, 88 monthlies and 26 quarterlies for London alone. Many were religious journals, but the range of opinion was extraordinarily wide, from sensational literature and scurrilous Tory sheets to the Radical journals of William Cobbett and Richard Carlile. In between were the sober, heavyweight middle-class journals whose purposes were the elabo-ration of a bourgeois philosophy suited and adapted to the aims and objectives of a successful and rapidly developing industrial society. By the mid-1830s middle-class consciousness was founded upon a clear understanding of the requirements of bourgeois property and a firm appreciation of the political obstacles and institutions that were delaying progress.

By the beginning of the nineteenth century merchants and bankers had been at work, and acquiring wealth, for a very long time. The new men in 1800 were the industrial capitalists, among whom the great cotton- and ironmasters were outstanding. Richard Arkwright began with no capital assets; his fame as an inventor rests upon somewhat doubtful ground, but his extraordinary capacity for financial matters and his great managerial abilities made him the first great 'cotton lord'. When he died in 1792 he left about £500,000; but when his son died in 1843 his personal wealth can be accurately estimated at £2,227,650, and this in addition to his real estate, whose values did not enter the Death Duty Registers until 1853. The Arkwrights were among the new rich, not yet at all equal to the fortunes of the landed aristocracy or even of some of the mercantile groups; but industrial capitalism was still in its first half century of development, and the industry state was already in being – and growing fast.

CHAPTER 4

Aristocracy and Bourgeois: the Sharing of Power

At the time of the revolution of 1688 there were about 160 peers, and their numbers slowly increased between then and the accession of George III in 1760. There followed an accelerated growth in the total of those legally entitled to sit in the House of Lords, a relatively slow increase at first but one that later rose sharply. The Union with Ireland in 1801 added 28 representative Irish peers and four spiritual Lords. Between 1783 and 1833 the number of peers who could vote in the Lords nearly doubled, from 230 to 423. In 1847 the number was 450 and in 1867 it was 464: figures, it should be noted, to be regarded only as approximate. During this period of growth in numbers there was also a change in the social composition of the nobility. Until about the last quarter of the eighteenth century titles given to the nobility had been the exclusive property of English grandees, almost always related to ownership of land, but from about the 1790s the peerage was now extended to those who had distinguished themselves – according to contemporary definition – in the public service: as diplomats, soldiers, judges and politicians. Most were still connected with land or families with landed property. Those still not ennobled were the representatives of commerce and industry, although by the 1830s the occasional knighthood was being granted. This general increase in the numbers allowed to vote in the House of Lords strengthened the Tory majority, a political position enhanced by the introduction of Irish peers after 1801.

Throughout the eighteenth century and down to 1832 the landed aristocracy in the House of Lords, and their sons and relatives and the gentry in the Commons, gathered to themselves all the political and administrative offices of government and the country in general. This assembly of power and positions included a massive trawl of government finances for their own benefit and for use in widespread patronage, not least among their own relatives. 'Old Corruption', it came to be called; the description of its practices, and bitter criticism of its operations, was at the centre of Radicalism after 1815, with William Cobbett as one of its most vigorous denouncers.

An Act of 1711 defined the qualifications for membership of the House of Commons. County members were required to have an income of £600 per annum from freehold or copyhold lands, and a borough member an income of £300. There were some exceptions, but the original purpose of this legislation was to restrict the growing influence of what Jonathan Swift had described as 'the monied interest'. The Qualification Bill, as it was known, was often ignored or circumvented, and many MPs in the next 100 years were elected on fictitious qualifications. In 1838 the law was amended to include personal property as well as real estate, but property qualifications for membership were not abolished until 20 years later. More important was the control over constituencies exercised by patrons: the government, the landed classes and, to a lesser extent, the Established Church. Each English county sent two members to the Commons and the right to vote in the counties was restricted to the 40-shilling freeholders. In the urban boroughs the qualifications were extraordinarily varied and complex. Some borough electorates approached household suffrage, but many parliamentary seats had small, sometimes very small numbers of electors; most of these were 'rotten' or 'pocket' boroughs controlled by one of the large landowners. In the early nineteenth century Cornwall, for example, had 21 borough seats, each with less than 200 electors. The five counties of the south-west of England elected a quarter of the total membership of the House of Commons, while the large growing towns of Manchester, Birmingham, Leeds and Sheffield were unrepresented. Scotland was even more restricted, with much higher property qualifications for the right to vote. Just before the Reform Bill of 1832, when Scotland's population was over 2.25 million, its total electorate was around 4,500. It was estimated that about half the membership of the House of Commons owed their seats to patrons.

The effective movement for parliamentary reform began with John Wilkes and Christopher Wyvill in the later decades of the eighteenth century, but the 1789 revolution ended what few developments there had been; only after the Treaty of Amiens (1802) did the Reform agitation become active again, still in a quite minor key. It was, however, to develop actively once the wars with France ended, and a major component of what was to become a nationwide agitation was the attack upon Old Corruption. John Wade in 1820 published his *Extraordinary Black Book*, followed by new and enlarged editions in 1832. He brought together in these pages all the abuses and corrupt practices he could discover from official sources; the list of persons who benefited ran into many hundreds. The 1832 *Black Book* is a remarkable compilation, and while Old Corruption was already gradually being eliminated or cut back, the details Wade produced were evidence of the breadth and depth of the place of the landed classes in British society and of the large-scale financial benefits that they and their families received from the national revenue. The Established Church had its own privileged place within this framework of corruption. It was, as Halévy remarked, 'a branch of the aristocracy' and an extremely heavy charge upon public finances. An official estimate put the subventions at £3.5 million a year, although critics put the total much higher. Even more scandalous was the Church of Ireland, a Protestant imposition upon a population that was overwhelmingly Catholic. Wade calculated that in 1832 the revenues of the Church of Ireland were just under £1.5 million, of which the money from tithes reached nearly £600,000. The average income of the Protestant Irish bishops he put at around £10,000 each. Many of them were absentees for a large part of the year.

Wade produced an alphabetical list of salaries, pensions, sinecures and so on, covering as many individuals for whom detail could be found. His list was corrected to February 1832 and to a number of names he appended explanatory comment. Thus:

Grafton, duke of, hereditary pension out of excise revenue	£7,200
Ditto, ditto post-office ditto	£4,700
Sealer of King's bench and common pleas	£2,888

One of the four illegitimate descendants of Charles II, raised to ducal peerages. It might be right in this profligate king to quarter the produce of his debauchery on the people's industry, but it is with surprise and indignation we find it continued to the present day. How happened it the revolution Whigs of 1688 did not rid the country of this infamy? The present duke returns two or three members to the lower house: he is said to be an 'excellent gentleman'; whether the motto – *Et decus et pretium recti* – 'the ornament and recompense of virtue' refers to the pensions or the descent of his grace is not easy to determine.

Elsewhere in the *Black Book* Wade commented on the Duke of Grafton's position as sealer in the King's Bench, for which the emoluments were £2,888: 'though we dare say his grace never sealed a writ in his life, nor ever once entered the dark and dirty hole in Inner Temple Lane, where that function is performed by his representative'.

The ferocious attacks upon this aristocratic Establishment by the middle-class reformers of the *Westminster Review* and the vigorous artisanal Radicalism which found its most comprehensive expression in the *Poor Man's Guardian* of the early 1830s – only one of a great flowering of the working-class press in these years – all came together to encourage the rapidly growing movement for parliamentary reform. The crisis of the Reform movement came between 1 March 1831, when Lord John Russell introduced the first Reform Bill, and June 1832, when in its final version the Bill received a very grudging Royal assent. The period during which the reform measures were being debated saw months of widespread violence throughout many parts of the country. There was serious economic distress in certain areas; the Swing riots of the summer and autumn of 1830 continued into the autumn of 1831 and swept through the southern agricultural counties; and following the rejection by the Lords of the second version of the Reform Bill in October 1831 there were outbreaks of large-scale violence in a number of towns, notably Nottingham and Bristol. The French Revolution of the summer of 1830 had further encouraged radical sentiment in Britain, and all over the country political unions were being established, founded on the model of the Birmingham Political Union. The most lively and extensive Radical organisation in London, with some offshoots in other parts of the country, was the National Union of the Working Classes, established in the spring of 1831. Between November 1830 and March 1831 Parliament received over 600 petitions in favour of the Reform Bill. Without question there was a massive popular sentiment for change, and among the traditional ruling groups there was apprehension which for some was unalleviated fear. Sir William Napier, at times an advanced Liberal, wrote to his wife in January 1831: 'before spring all Europe will be in war and turmoil. Here in London men speak sedition openly in the clubs and secretly in the streets; every person is prepared or preparing for a great change'. In late February he warned his wife and daughter to get ready for exile.

Historians have differed concerning the revolutionary potential of the Reform agitation. There was a great deal of rioting, and considerable violence; the sentiment for change was widespread; and to many contemporary observers the possibilities of joint action between the middle classes and the working people seemed both possible and desperately ominous. There are no set formulas for revolutions, although there are certain necessary conditions for revolution within a modern or a modernising society. One is that the ruling class or the dominant sections within the ruling groups should no longer be able to maintain control, and in particular should be weak in organising and using the coercive powers of the state. There is no doubt that the security forces at the disposal of the British governments of 1831–2 were not as well organised as they later became in the 1840s, and before the age of the railway it was a fairly slow business switching troops from one part of the country to another. Only London had a police force of any significance, but it was still inexperienced in riot control. There was the Yeomanry, of course, but no government, especially a Whig administration, wanted to risk a repetition of the Peterloo massacre. Nevertheless, there is no suggestion from Home Office papers and other correspondence that the Home Secretary and his handful of senior officials were ever in doubt about their ability to control events. There is the further, important question of the willingness of the middle-class reformers to go beyond their rhetoric and actually engage in physical force. They might indeed have 'Gone for Gold' in an attempt to destabilise the general situation, but to believe they would have fought on the streets alongside a mixture of the respectable artisans and the 'common' labourers is surely pushing political credulity somewhat. In the last resort they believed the integrity of the existing state of society must be preserved whatever the human cost, and there is no hard evidence that the traditional ruling classes, the landed classes as a whole, were ready to walk away from what they regarded as their rightful inheritance.

The Whig ministry which carried the Reform Act was careful not to concede more than was politically necessary in the conditions of the time. Indeed the details of the Reform measures illustrate vividly how conservative political and social change in Britain has been over the past two centuries. The total number of parliamentary seats remained the same after 1832. Fifty-six of the smaller English boroughs were completely disfranchised, while 30 others lost one of their two members. Twenty-two new parliamentary boroughs were created with two members each, and 19 more with one member. The county representation was increased. In Scotland the pattern was similar to that in England. County seats were unchanged at 30 seats and borough representation increased from 15 to 23. Edinburgh and Glasgow each returned two members and other large towns one member. The general result of redistribution was to give representation to the industrial towns for the first time, and these of course were mainly in the north of England. There remained many anomalies in the relationship between the size of electorates and number of parliamentary seats, and these were especially marked between different parts of Britain. The agricultural south of England, grossly over-represented before 1832, still had a higher proportion of seats, considering the size of its population, than elsewhere. There were many ways in which the landed interest offset the influence of the urban middle class. Many country towns which belonged more to the rural than the urban sector retained their representation and their constituency boundaries were extended into the surrounding countryside. Any growth in the urban centres would therefore be offset by the rural vote. Moreover, as already noted, there was a marked increase in the number of county members.

Voting qualifications under the new Act gave a uniform franchise in the boroughs. Those who occupied buildings of an annual value of £10, whether as tenant or owner, were now enfranchised provided they had twelve months' residence and had paid their rates and taxes. In the English counties matters were complex, but it was the social groups above that of the agricultural labourer who obtained the vote. In the urban boroughs some skilled workers might reach the £10 householder level, but the overwhelming mass of the new voters were middle or lower middle class. Before 1832 the electorate had numbered about 478,000; now, under the Reform provisions, the figure was 813,000. As Lord John Russell said in the House of Commons in November 1837:

> at the time the Reform Bill was passed, I stated my belief that it must necessarily give a preponderance to the landed interest; and although it may be deemed that such a preponderance has been somewhat unduly given, I still think that a preponderance in favour of that interest tends to the stability of the general institutions of the country.

The historian Macaulay had made the same point in one of the speeches after the Reform Bill was first discussed. On 2 March 1831 he had insisted that 'I support this measure as a measure of reform; but I support it still more as a measure of conservation.' 'Reform, that you may preserve', he said in the same speech.

The significance of 1832 must not, however, be underestimated. The Reform Act left political power in the hands of the traditional ruling class, the landed interests. They dominated the two Houses of Parliament; they continued to provide the membership of Cabinets in both Whig and Tory governments; they still controlled the patronage of the administration in Whitehall; and the Established Church and the armed forces remained untouched. Economic, social and administrative changes were, however, already in train and would lead society to adapt to the political and social requirements of the developing capitalist order.

There was a political complement to the 1832 Reform Act whose significance is often overlooked, but whose passing was the necessary extension of the Act. This was the 1835 Municipal Corporations Act, which made over to the wealthier sections of the middle classes the political control of their own towns. The county system had previously been (and was to remain) a government by the local landed classes, while the boroughs were controlled by privileged corporations, mostly responsible to no one save themselves. The passing of the Reform Act meant that these corporations were no longer able to choose parliamentary members, or to control the elections to Parliament, and their entrenched corrupt practices now became matters of public debate. The Whig government set up a

Select Committee in 1833 to enquire into the administration of municipal boroughs, but its powers and resources were inadequate. Accordingly the government followed the precedent of the Poor Law inquiry and established a Royal Commission, composed mainly of young barristers, most of whom had Whig sympathies. On 30 March 1835 there appeared a Report with five great appendices, the whole occupying 3,446 pages of print.

The general conclusions, and the mass of evidence, characterised the existing municipal corporations as grossly inefficient almost everywhere, and thoroughly corrupt in a majority of boroughs. *The Times* had spoken of the 'chartered hogsties', and the Royal Commission fleshed out this generalisation in immense detail. The old corporations were controlled by the freemen, whose numbers could range from a dozen or so to 5,000. The powers of the corporations were exercised by the common councils, which in a few boroughs were elected by the freemen but which in most were self-perpetuating. The main prerogative of the freemen, before the Reform Act of 1832, was to vote for the parliamentary candidates, by whom it was normal to be entertained, or paid, or both. The common council looked after the property of the corporation – which could be considerable – and although the experience of boroughs varied greatly, the great majority practised the arts of fraud, jobbery and venality with the self-confidence of the inheritors of a long and dishonourable tradition.

The Report of the Commission recommended the transfer of corporation property – which hitherto had been recognised by equity lawyers as equivalent to the property of private individuals – to borough councils which would be elected on the basis of complete household suffrage. The councils were to use corporation property only for the benefit of the public. It was these sweeping changes, embodied in a Municipal Corporations Act that was produced within a month of the publication of the Report, that for many Tories were even more sinister in their political implications than the 1832 Reform Act. The Corporations Bill went through the Commons with only minor changes, a matter of grave concern to the Tories in the House of Lords, who mustered their forces behind the Duke of Wellington in fighting spirit. The Act finally emerged in what one historian has described as a 'much chastened form', by which was meant the elimination of the more democratic clauses of the Bill. Nevertheless, the important shifts in political power remained. The borough government now became representative not of the freemen but of the burgesses; that is, of all the ratepayers of the borough. The council of the borough was composed of councillors, who made up three-quarters of the total, and of aldermen who were elected by members of the council. The mayor was also elected by the council. There was no property qualification for those who stood as candidates, except the ratepaying clause.

The Act applied to only 179 boroughs, and incorporation, which meant the acceptance of the new rules and regulations, was not automatic. The timing of incorporation, based as it was on the vote of the ratepayers, depended upon the balance of political force within the borough. Bradford, for example, was denied incorporation for over a decade, the result of a political combination of Tories and working-class Chartists. In all the large towns after incorporation the first elections produced Whig/Liberal majorities. In Manchester and Birmingham, for instance, at their first elections in 1838 not a single Tory was returned. The year 1848 was among the most turbulent of the first half of the century. The northern towns which in that year were racked by problems of riot and widespread agitation – Manchester, Bradford, Leeds – together with Birmingham in the Midlands, all had middle-class Liberal mayors. Only Liverpool, beset with religious sectarianism, was the exception. In sum, in this crucial historical year the Whig aristocracy ruled at Westminster, and its provincial middle-class allies dominated the great town halls.

During the first half of the nineteenth century Britain was moving steadily towards becoming an advanced capitalist society, and those who were using capital for economic development, in all its many forms, were fast becoming wealthier and more powerful. As a result of the Reform Act of 1832 and the Municipal Corporations Act of 1835, together with the legal and institutional changes that have been discussed in these pages, the commercial and industrial bourgeoisie was beginning to move towards the centre of political power. The political history of the second half of the nineteenth century can be read in these terms, although naturally the story is one of multiple and complex trends.

An essential part of this analysis concerns the landed classes, and in particular how they continued to maintain their powerful position in British society for so long. The answers are intricate, the reasons complicated, and yet there is a two-sided generalisation that provides the starting point for any analysis. The first part is that which notes the weight and importance of tradition, of the ways in which the landed classes had become deeply embedded in society, and the difficulties any reforming movement has, in any society of this kind – and of many other kinds – in effecting change. The second part can be quite straightforwardly expressed: indus-trialisation proved to be a very profitable development for the landed classes. The possession of the land of the country was an enormous asset that steadily, with industrial growth, became more and more financially worthwhile.

Analysis must therefore begin with the ways in which the landed classes held on to their land through succeeding generations. By about 1700 the landed classes had obtained all the necessary requirements upon which their economic and political power in the eighteenth century (so well illustrated by the country house-building of these years) was to be consolidated and from which base it was to be so steadily expanded. The threat of a Papist monarchy was virtually gone; there were no hindrances of any major kind to the expansion of their holdings at the expense of the small owners; and they now had, through the legal devices of strict settlement, ways in which the family estates could be maintained more or less intact through succeeding heirs and their families.

The concentration of landownership needs emphasis. While the fact that concentration occurred in the nineteenth century is not denied, there is still argument about the changes over time. What is certainly accepted is the long-term trend of the growing importance of the large estate. The conveyancing procedures known as strict settlement were first elaborated in more or less their eighteenth- and nineteenth-century forms in the decades following the Restoration of 1660. There were different kinds of settlement and they could be agreed on marriage of the heir, by will or when the person named as tenant in tail came of age. The intended conse-quences of this practice of ensuring the continuation of the family estate through future generations were not always achieved as some landed families were crushed by debt and forced sales, but the great majority survived and flourished. We have no accurate data on landholding until the 1870s and the official *Return of Owners of Land*. The raw data of this national survey had to be con-siderably reworked, but the broad conclusions were indisputable. London was excluded from the survey, as were some other categories of rural land, but on the adjusted data it was estimated that about a quarter of the land of the United Kingdom was owned by 1,200 persons and about half by 7,400. What the figures were in 1800 is not known with any precision, but it is reasonable to assume that concentration of ownership then, while not necessarily as marked as in the 1870s, was nevertheless considerable. It was this ownership of land that provided the aristocracy and the gentry with their rising rent-rolls. Agriculture, except in only a few years, was a profitable business in the nineteenth century until the late 1870s, and the years of 'High Farming' in the middle decades of the century continued the long-term secular improvement in farming profits and rents.

In English law the ownership of land conferred rights not only to the soil worked for agricultural purposes but to everything beneath the surface; thus with coal as the growing source of energy from the late eighteenth century onwards, landowners with coal beneath their lands found themselves with remarkable increases in their incomes. To give one example, the wife of the Marquis of Londonderry, the only child of Sir Henry Vane Tempest, inherited very large properties in the county of Durham which in time became studded with collieries. Londonderry himself had sharp entrepreneurial abilities, and among many other activities relating to his mining interests he was largely responsible for building the seaport of Seaham for coal shipments. Right round Britain where there were coal reserves the pattern was repeated. Some landowners assumed direct control over the working of their own mines, but the general trend over time was to lease and take royalties.

Ownership of land provided many other returns too. Industrialisation meant urbanisation, and in a geographically small country like Britain the growth of many towns offered major rewards to those who became urban landlords. London rents, of course, were the most profitable, and the Dukes of Bedford, Portland, Norfolk and Westminster were only the largest beneficiaries among many. Railway building over aristocratic property was a further and important source of money. Thus we have the rise in the value of agricultural rentals until about 1880, royalties from mining and quarrying, wayleaves from the carriage of goods over land, urban rents from the uninterrupted growth of towns and their suburbs, income or capital from railway development: it is hardly surprising that for so long the landed classes remained the richest group in an industrialising Britain. And given who these people were, the financial returns they reaped from government and administrative office were by no means inconsiderable, in spite of the elimination – which was never complete – of the worst abuses of Old Corruption before 1850. The possibilities, too, of enlarging the capital base of the landed family, either through straight investment or through entrepreneurial activity of some kind, were always present and usually acted upon. What is odd is that some historians have advertised their surprise that the landed classes steadily increased their wealth and remained so rich in an economy that was being remodelled from its traditional agrarian base.

The matters itemised here have taken no account of the ownership of land in Ireland. The conquest of Ireland had been more or less completed during the reign of Elizabeth, and until the Union with Britain in 1800 Ireland remained a colony ruled from Dublin in the interests of the English propertied classes. As a result of the depredations of the seventeenth century, Irish Catholics were in possession of only 14 per cent of the productive land of their country at the beginning of the next century. The overwhelming mass of the peasantry lived in bitter, degrading poverty, and although the economy began to improve after the mid-eighteenth century, the mutilating lifestyles of the labouring people were only slowly remedied; even in Ulster living standards by the end of the century bore no comparison with those in England. Before the 1780s there were almost insuperable problems for Catholics in the matter of personal advancement; and the Union of 1800–1 – the product of political bargaining, lying promises and massive corruption – brought only very slow improvement in the economic and political position of the Catholic population. The colonial relationship was never completely altered, and English landlords continued their exploitation of the Irish peasantry. The drain of capital out of Ireland – from rents, the revenues of the Anglican Church, a massive bureaucracy largely staffed at its senior levels by the English, and an extended Pension List that paid out to those who had served more than a month in Ireland – was a helpful contribution to the stream of English accumulation before the period of industrialisation proper. This was all part of the grim record over the centuries which developed the sense of history as injustice that became such a marked characteristic of Irish consciousness in the period of nationalism.

The Union with Ireland brought certain changes of emphasis within the British Parliament in that Irish affairs now received a good deal more attention than hitherto. The Union had added 100 Irish MPs to the Commons, and it was directly and indirectly responsible for strengthening the Irish landed interest in the House of Lords. There was now a specifically Orange group in the Lords, reactionaries in Irish affairs and unpleasant in all other matters. A further trend which worked in the same direction was the general increase in the total number of peers sitting in the House. Until around 1780 about one-eighth of all peers in the Lords had some Irish interest – ownership of land or mortgages or a pension – but by the early 1830s almost one in four possessed an 'Irish interest'; and as a general rule, ownership of land in Ireland, or some specific interest, tended to encourage right-wing attitudes beyond the average. If we take again the year 1848 – that critical year for English politics – two of the three leading Whigs in government had a strong Irish interest. Palmerston had inherited 6,000 acres in Ireland, and probably half his income for many years of his life came from Irish rents. The Marquis of Lansdowne, Lord President of the Council, had considerable estates in both England and Scotland; his Irish acreage was over 100,000. Only Lord John Russell had no direct Irish connections.

A necessary condition for industrial development in Britain was the liberalisation of trade policies. As the first industrial society, Britain was in a commanding position to export manufactured goods, both to nations who were at their own first stage of industrialisation and also to the primary producing areas of the world which were already exporting their raw materials to Britain and the newly industrialising societies. The continued domination of the landed classes in Britain after the legislative changes of the 1830s was accompanied by a dismantling of the restrictions upon international trade inherited from the eighteenth century. The Corn Law of 1815, imposed directly in the interests of the landlord classes, led to the vigorous reactions of the 1840s, but already in the 1820s Huskisson and his colleagues had begun the processes through which free trade would ultimately be realised. The free trade question had been somewhat overshadowed by the reform legislation, but the formation of the Anti-Corn Law League in 1838, with Cobden and Bright as its main spokesmen, reflected the middle classes' growing confidence in their political and social positions in society. It gave a clear warning to agricultural interests that the balance of economic power was shifting steadily towards the commercial and industrial sectors.

The Conservative government of Peel continued the policy of trade liberalisation. Peel himself had already agreed in a speech in 1842 upon 'the general principle of free trade … that we should purchase in the cheapest market and sell in the dearest'; and his government's first Budgets had abolished most of the duties on the raw materials of manufacturing industry and reduced the import duties on some 750 items on the customs list. Preferential treatment was given to colonial produce. The central problem, however, for the advocates of free trade was the import restrictions on grain. The failure of the wheat crop in 1845 and the simultaneous blight on Irish potatoes meant that by the autumn of 1845 it was evident Ireland was at the beginning of a serious famine which over the next three years became the greatest social catastrophe of nineteenth-century Europe. The political controversies following Peel's public announcement of Corn Law repeal need not detain us. The Conservative Party splintered and the Whigs came to power under Lord John Russell at the end of July 1846. The political and economic arguments on both sides were exaggerated in that the consequences for the agricultural interest were not felt for another three decades. What was not exaggerated was the cataclysm of the famine in Ireland, with whose consequences the Parliament at Westminster proved wholly incapable of coping: a grievous example of the triumph of ignorant dogma over commonsense and compassion.

The real meaning of the greatly overplayed drama of the English Corn Laws was the middle classes' insistence upon their place in society through this exhibition of their political strength. Yet just as the landed groups had to recognise the political economy of the business world as the essential basis of British wealth and prosperity, so the middle classes were forced to accept the continuation of aristocratic domination in many parts of the political structure At Westminster the aristocracy still sat in the seats of power; at Lambeth Palace the Archbishop of Canterbury continued to preside over an Established Church whose privileges had not in any way been curtailed. The Diplomatic Service remained an aristocratic preserve for the rest of the century and well beyond; the home Civil Service, reformed in the mid-1850s, continued to recruit its entrants from the public schools, especially those of the old foundations. In the long run the various factions of the propertied classes came together in a symbiosis which produced in the Tory Party the most effective political organisation of the twentieth century.

Already, by the first half of the nineteenth century, there was taking place a commingling of some landed Tories and groups with the business interests of the middle classes. One reflection of this was the support given by certain Tory landowners to Corn Law repeal; another was the general acceptance at home of laissez-faire as the general principle upon which business affairs should be conducted. In 1848 the unanimity with which the British press denounced the impracticality of French social ideas and upheld the wisdom of economic freedom in Britain, was quite remarkable. On 3 March 1848 the British Ambassador to France, the Marquis of Normanby, summarised for Palmerston a discussion he had had with Lamartine, the French Foreign Secretary in the Provisional government:

> He must be aware that in a country like England its complicated interests were all bound together by the security derived from the protection of capital and its free employment, and therefore there were some of the former doctrines of one of his present colleagues, Louis Blanc, which some were afraid appeared likely to be put into practice.

CHAPTER 5

Internal Security: Persons and Property

Britain in the eighteenth century was a society experiencing sustained economic growth, a rapid increase of population and a growing rate of urbanisation in the closing decades, a continuing enfeeblement of traditional social structures, and a notable growth in the number of acts of robbery and violence against the person as well as property. The marked tendency of large numbers of ordinary people to engage in riotous behaviour encouraged other countries in Europe to regard the British as 'ungovernable'.

The number of indictable offences, especially for stealing and robbery, which were punishable by hanging extended dramatically during the eighteenth century. Crime grew with population, and nowhere more obviously than in London, which by 1800 was approaching the one million mark. London was not only the centre of government and the city where most of the landed aristocracy had town houses, it was also the most important centre of commercial activity and of much manufacturing industry, mostly of the independent artisan and small master type. What happened in London was of immediate concern to leading politicians and the social elites. There was a marked increase in the range and number of private security arrangements as well as those established under official auspices. But the stipendiary magistrates' police, formed in 1782, and the Bow Street Runners, set up in the mid-eighteenth century, became steeped in corruption, while the Thames Police, who supervised the loading and unloading of cargoes at the docks, were among the relatively honest custodians. Inevitably in the country as a whole, when confronted with the riotous masses, the army was the only really effective method of control, and for a number of reasons this was clearly not satisfactory. Successive governments, from about the last quarter of the century onwards, tried to meet their growing security problems with more satisfactory methods, against a background of rapid social change that was yearly adding to the scale of crime and its attendant violence.

Governments at Westminster were faced with two separate but closely related problems. One was the internal security of mainland Britain and especially of the large and growing towns; the second, so often marginalised in English historical writing, comprised the problems of England's oldest colony, Ireland. The history of Ireland is not, for the most part, an obtrusive element in English social and political consciousness; the facts of history, that for centuries under English rule the overwhelming mass of the Irish peasantry lived in degrading poverty, do not come immediately into English minds when Ireland is discussed. It was a poverty beyond that experienced by the most depressed classes on the mainland; and throughout the first half of the nineteenth century social and personal crime in the province was on levels that sharply distinguished Ireland from the rest of the United Kingdom. In many areas violence against both the person and property was a daily occurrence. Discontent was endemic and there was serious rural unrest after the Union, with many different protest movements according to locality, often generalised under the name 'Whiteboys'.

There was much to be protected. As already noted, many English landed aristocrats had considerable estates in Ireland; there was a steady financial drain of capital from a lengthy Pension List, and lavish payments to members of the Established Church. Of the last-named John Wade, in his 1832 edition of the *Black Book*, wrote in blunt and precise terms:

> The Irish branch of the United Church [that is, the Established Church of England and Ireland] is more pregnant with abuses even than its sister establishment in England; presenting a more revolting spectacle of inordinate incomes, of lax discipline, of laborious duties without adequate remuneration, and of an immense ecclesiastical revenue levied under circumstances of greater insult, partiality, and oppression.

The problems of security in Ireland were therefore different in scale but closely connected with those on the mainland. For one thing the location of the regiments of the army had to take into account the relevant levels of violence in Ireland and the mainland. Military resources were limited and the movement of troops before the railway age was always slow and cumbersome. If there were serious disturbances simultaneously in Ireland and on the mainland, then the problems of allocation would be considerable; on a less significant level, but still a matter of importance, the ethnic composition of regiments had also to be taken into account. English troops set against Irish Catholic peasants would be no problem, but if there were only Irish regiments available for the task then there might be disquiet. In general, it needs to be said that while there were problems of this kind during the decades leading up to 1848, they were never of a critical kind, largely it may be surmised because the problems were always appreciated when assignments were being made.

The degree of brutality practised by those in authority in Ireland, as well as the violence that suffused many actions of the peasantry, had no counterpart in other areas of Britain, but the organisation of measures of security contained lessons for those on the mainland. The introduction of new methods came earlier in Ireland. After Robert Peel became Chief Secretary at Dublin Castle in 1812 he introduced a new mobile police force to supplement the traditional baronial police who were underpaid, often part-time and mostly ineffective. Peel's new Peace Preservation Force consisted of specially selected police constables whom the Lord Lieutenant (the 'Viceroy') in Dublin could send to any area 'proclaimed' because of emergency conditions; and accompanying the police would be a Chief Magistrate who would take precedence over the local JPs. The Chief Magistrate, an essential part of the Peelite reform, was paid £700 a year while the lowest rank of sub-constable received £50 a year, a salary considerably higher than the payment made to the old baronial police. The costs of the Peace Preservation Force when despatched to a troubled region were met by the area they were stationed in. The system developed by Peel evolved into a national Irish constabulary by the 1830s.

The requirements of policing in Ireland must be clearly outlined. Ireland had been an occupied country for centuries, with the majority of the population adherents of a religion which was also the religion of the main enemies of Britain: Spain and France. There was always an important strategic component within British attitudes towards Ireland, although the proprietary interest of the English landed classes was the most important single factor. Given the colonial relationship, much exacerbated by the difference in religion, the nature and character of policing in Ireland had to be different in a number of ways from that practised in England. In the first place the control of the security forces had to be centralised in Dublin, since there were no trustworthy local groups comparable with the English Justices of the Peace (recruited from the local gentry or the Anglican Church). In Ireland those eligible for the magistracy were Protestants within a population that was overwhelmingly Catholic, except in parts of Ulster, and where there was bitter hatred in the countryside. Those involved in law and order in Ireland lived and worked in a hostile environment, and they had to be armed. Ireland therefore obtained, when the administrative reforms were completed, a highly centralised police force organised on paramilitary lines. Constables and sergeants lived in barracks away from the contamination of their fellow citizens. Constables were never stationed in their home region. That had been formerly tried, explained Major-General Sir Duncan MacGregor to a Select Committee of the House of Lords in 1854, but had been found to be 'pernicious'. The paramilitary character of the Irish police needs to be emphasised, as does the hostility of the mass of the population towards the police. Outside observers were always struck by the omnipresence of the police in both town and country. In 1847 Alexander Somerville set down his impressions:

> One of the first things which attract the eye of a stranger in Ireland, at least such a stranger as I am, and make him halt in his steps and turn around and look, is the police whom he meets in every part of the island, and on every road, and in every village, even on the farm land, and on the seashore, and on the little islands which lie out in the sea. These policemen wear a dark green uniform and are armed; this is what makes them remarkable, armed from the heel to the head. They have belts and pouches, ball cartridges in the pouches, short guns called carbines, and bayonets, and pistols, and swords. The only difference between them and the regular military is, that the regular military do not always carry guns and pistols primed and loaded, not always bayonets in their belts, not always swords sharpened. The Irish police never go on duty without some of these.

A few years later Friedrich Engels wrote to Marx in the same terms, to the effect that he 'had never seen so many gendarmes in any country, and the sodden look of the bibulous Prussian gendarme is developed to its highest perfection here among the constabulary, who are armed with carbine, bayonets and handcuffs'.

There were some attempts by the Whig administration in the middle years of the 1830s to lessen or modify the sectarian character of the Irish police force. It had traditionally been recruited from the Protestant section of the population and Orange ideas were widespread. The 1836 Act prohibited police officers from being members of secret societies – with one exception, the Freemasons, who were excluded from the prohibition because Freemasonry, so it was suggested, was 'largely charitable'. This, of course, has always been the claim of Freemasons in Britain, and certainly there has rarely been a comparison with the political sectarianism of the Masonic movement in parts of Europe. In Ireland, however, while Roman Catholics had been members of Masonic lodges in the eighteenth century in spite of the Papal Bull of 1738 which condemned Freemasonry and banned membership by Catholics, it was only in the closing years of the century and in the early nineteenth century that Irish Catholics withdrew from Freemasonry. By 1836 it is improbable that there were any Catholics left in the Masonic lodges, and the effect therefore of the exception clause would have meant that the lodges were Protestant and, it may be suggested without straining the argument, more strongly anti-Catholic than in many parts of mainland Britain. There is a further consideration. Freemasonry has always been a middle- and upper-class movement in Britain. Some working-class lodges did grow during the nineteenth century, but overwhelmingly Masonic lodges were conservative institutions where businessmen and politicians and professional people were able to talk over their affairs and without doubt 'help' each other; this was the case at all levels, from the small provincial town to the elitist lodges of London and the major cities.

Now in Ireland the officers of the police force were for the most part not recruited from the ranks, as they were in Britain, except for the very top positions. They came from the ranks of the 'gentlemen'. An enquiry in 1866 into the pay and qualifications of the Irish constabulary made the point that it was not possible to compare the lower and middle ranks of the police officers in Ireland with those in the rest of Britain. The comparison could only be with the officer class in the British army, whose members, with few exceptions, were always 'of gentle birth'. In Ireland, the Report noted, officers came into close contact with the gentry of their counties and it was essential that they should be of the social position which would enable them to associate on equal terms.

As in the rest of Britain, there was provision for the enrolment of special constables, but given the small number of the middle classes, in town and country, who could be expected to be friendly to the administration in Dublin Castle, their role was never important. By an Act of 1832, it should be noted, special constables were entitled to all the privileges of the professional police, including the carrying of arms: something which was never, at any period, allowed in Britain however serious the local situation.

Internal security in mainland Britain during the eighteenth century and until the reforms of the late 1820s still relied mainly upon the traditional structure of local government suitable for a mostly rural society of villages and small country towns. With the growth of population and the increasing density of manufacturing industry, the scale of the general problem was changing. There were some reforms before 1800, but there was a quite remarkable reluctance on the part of Parliament to consider seriously the organisation of a professional police force on a national basis. The essential fallback for those responsible for law and order remained the military.

The authority responsible for the keeping of the King's Peace, the legal phrase for the normal state of society, consisted of the King's Ministers. In practice this meant the Secretary of State at the Home Office. While the Viceroy in Dublin was responsible for Ireland, in the last resort he was subordinate to the Home Secretary in Whitehall. The Home Secretary appointed, on behalf of the Crown, the Lord Lieutenant of each county, always chosen from the landed aristocracy and normally the leader of the social life of the propertied classes, although not necessarily those involved in trade or manufacturing. The appointments of Vice-Lieutenants and country magistrates were made on their recommendation, and in the event of disorder of any kind it was the responsibility of the Lord Lieutenant to provide leadership. The county Yeomanry was under his direct control.

Not all Lords Lieutenant accepted their duties. Some did not live in the county over which they had charge and some were incapacitated. In the Lord Lieutenant's absence the Vice-Lieutenant could take over, although such action was not universal. It was the magistracy upon whom most of the burden of maintaining order rested, although again not all magistrates accepted their responsibilities. There were property qualifications to be met before appointment, but these were set low enough for quite small landowners to be eligible. The problems of recruitment were often serious, for the gentry frequently showed a marked reluctance to sit on the Bench. Moreover, there were political and social prejudices on the part of some Lords Lieutenant against the appointment of those outside the landed classes and the men of leisure. In 1839, for example, the Lord Lieutenant of Staffordshire rejected the appointment of a powder-blue manufacturer on the grounds that he never accepted anyone 'engaged in manufacture or trade in the district'.

In some regions there was a serious shortfall in the numbers and availability of magistrates. As Halévy wrote: 'as industry progressed, the country gentlemen fled'. During the early years of the second quarter of the nineteenth century there were about 5,000 magistrates in England, representing a doubling since the end of the seventeenth century, but an increase far lower than the rate of increase of the population as a whole. The problem was most acute in the large towns, industrial districts and mining regions. It was the difficulty of obtaining sufficient numbers of local Justices of the Peace that accounted for the growth in the presence of Anglican clergymen on the local Bench. The Webbs estimated that at about the time of the 1832 Reform Act one-quarter of the magistrates of England and Wales were Church of England priests. Eight English counties had a majority of clerical JPs and it was not until the third quarter of the century that the major fall in clerical representation occurred. In Warwickshire, for example, an increasingly industrial county, 40 per cent of magistrates in 1830 were clergymen, but this figure fell to seven per cent in 1868.

The magistrates were responsible for the maintenance of public order in their own area of jurisdiction. A disturbance that involved more than three people was a riot, and with more than twelve persons who refused to disperse the Riot Act of 1715 could be read. Once this had happened the riot became a felony, thereby allowing the local authorities to use force, including firearms. These decisions were the responsibility of the magistrates. It was their duty to gather a sufficient force and lead it in person to wherever the disturbance was located, and it was their decision whether the Riot Act should be read and whether, after this promulgation, fire could be ordered. For their immediate local security the magistrates had to rely upon their own police force, if any of its few members were available. Then, if necessary, two or more magistrates could swear in special constables, though it was never easy to find candidates. The magistrates could also, on their own initiatives, call out the local Yeomanry and they could require aid from the nearest military.

This last matter needs further explanation. The practice had grown up during the eighteenth century whereby the Secretary of State would issue a general order authorising military commanders to give aid to the civil power, and magistrates had become used to the practice of calling upon the military without first applying for permission to the Secretary of State. This precedent was accepted during the troubled decades of the first half of the nineteenth century, but it was always possible for the officer in charge of the military to whom the request was made either to refuse, on the grounds that the situation was not as serious as the magistrates thought or had indicated, or to refer the request to a superior officer.

The military forces in the United Kingdom were divided broadly between Ireland and mainland Britain, and their numerical distribution was related to the levels of disorder in these two regions at any one time. There was a constant shuffling of troops between Ireland and the rest of Britain. In 1839–40, for example, a time when there was relative tranquillity in Ireland but considerable levels of Chartist disturbances in Britain, there were about 27,000 troops in Britain and around 13,000 in Ireland. In 1848, by contrast, when Ireland was, or was thought to be, as disturbed as Britain, the number of troops was roughly equal in each region, a situation much helped by the largely fortuitous return to Britain of several regiments from overseas. In the 1840s there was a new factor of quite major significance: the growth of the railway network. In the mid-1840s a regiment could reach Manchester from London in nine hours; a journey on foot would have taken 17 days.

The military in Britain was divided into districts, the most important being commanded by senior generals, many of whom were Peninsular veterans. The largest district was the Northern Command, which was centred at Manchester and covered the whole of northern England, from the Scottish borders down to Birmingham and the counties of Leicestershire and Northamptonshire. When the military acted in support of the civil power it was in theory under the control of the civil authorities. The practice was not always in accord. At the Whitehall level the Home Secretary was responsible for the distribution of troops throughout Britain, although there was always consultation with the Horse Guards (that is, the War Office) and with the local military commanders. The latter, for the most part, were able and efficient and provided the Home Secretary with many of his most useful and informative reports on local situations.

Military officers were always concerned to remove their men from contact with local people and they deplored the absence of barrack accommodation, permanent or temporary. While some of the senior commanders discussed the likelihood of the political contamination of their troops by Radical groups during the 1830s and 1840s, there is no evidence that the military was in any way unreliable in this context. It was Ireland and the Irish which again provided more likely ground for possible disaffection. The British army always had a high proportion of Irishmen in its ranks, and from the 1830s onwards it is estimated that about one-third of the annual intake into the British army came from Ireland. Among the officer class Irish Protestants, especially from Ulster, were strongly represented. It was, of course, especially in Ireland that the question of loyalty among the rank and file was seriously discussed, but while there were a few incidents the Irish regiments proved as reliable as the rest of the army, in Ireland as elsewhere in Britain.

One factor that was important in the upholding of the army's morale was that it was rare – there were exceptions – for the army's intervention to be ineffective. The military commanders were conscious always of the political and psychological dangers which would follow if army detachments were overthrown at any time by the rioters, especially those of a Radical kind, and as far as possible the troops were always deployed in sufficient numbers. There were occasions during the Chartist years when troops were not used in riotous or potentially riotous situations because of the dangers that might follow if the detachments involved were of too small a size.

The years of peace after the ending of the Napoleonic Wars saw a gradual change in ruling-class opinion concerning the need for an adequate professional police on a nationwide basis. The social background was certainly tumultuous. The Luddite disturbances of 1811–12, the so-called Corn Law riots of 1815, the 'Pentridge Revolution' of 1817, the Peterloo killings of 1819 and the Cato Street conspiracy of 1820 were only the most sensational of the outbreaks of popular unrest in these years. The suspension of Habeas Corpus in 1817 and the passing of the Six Acts two years later were the response of a government that reflected the general alarm among the propertied classes, now buttressed by the awareness of political Radicalism that was finding increasing links with popular attitudes. What is interesting is the political reluctance at Westminster to accept the need for far-reaching changes in the administration of policing and the maintenance of internal security. A Committee of the House of Commons which sat for the years 1816–18 heard innumerable witnesses testifying to the extent and prevalence of crime, especially in London, and of the weaknesses in the legal system which encouraged corruption at all levels of society. Only in its third and last Report did the Committee consider the possibilities of a new kind of policing. Its final paragraph read:

> *Prevention of Crime.* This is a subject of great difficulty. It is no doubt true that to prevent crime is better than to punish it; but the difficulty is not in the end but in the means; and though your committee could imagine a system of police that might arrive at the object sought for, yet, in a free country, or even in one where any unrestrained intercourse of society is admitted, such a system would of necessity be odious and repulsive, and one which no government could be able to carry into execution. In despotic countries it has never yet succeeded to the extent aimed at by those theorists; and among a free people the very proposal would be rejected with abhorrence; it would be a plan which would make every servant of every house a spy of his master, and all classes spy on each other. The police of a free country is to be found in rational and humane laws – in an effective and enlightened magistracy – and in the judicious and proper selection of those officers of justice, in whose hands, as conservators of the peace, executive duties are legally placed.

Above all these considerations, the Committee went on, the security of a country rests upon 'The moral habits and opinions of the people'. It was possible that property might sometimes be 'invaded' or personal lives endangered, but what was crucial were those individual rights of each citizen which remain the central point of any free society.

These arguments were repeated some years later when Robert Peel, who had just succeeded Sidmouth as Home Secretary in 1822, set up a Committee with specific reference to the means whereby London could obtain 'as perfect a system of police as was consistent with the character of a free country'. In its Report the Committee underlined the moral approach of the 1818 conclusions:

> It is difficult to reconcile an effective system of police with that perfect freedom of action and exemption from interference which are the great privileges and blessing of society in this country; and Your Committee think that the forfeiture or curtailment of such advantages would be too great a sacrifice for improvements in police, or facilities in detection of crime, however desirable in themselves if abstractly considered.

Peel, temporarily rebuffed, continued to work for reforms and in 1828 he set up another Committee of Enquiry, this time with carefully selected members, and got what he wanted. In April 1829 he introduced a Bill for the creation of a metropolitan police force. His original Bill included the City of London, but by bowing to the storm of opposition this particular clause brought about he successfully persuaded the Whigs to accept the core of his proposals. As he wrote to the Duke of Wellington, he proposed to 'teach people that liberty does not consist of having your house robbed by organised gangs of thieves'.

Peel was clearly much influenced by his Irish experience, not least in making the London police responsible to the Home Office and not to the local authorities in the capital city. Although the police were not armed – that would have been impossible, given the political culture of late Georgian Britain – they were to be organised on a quasi-military basis with a simple teaching drill and the establishment of a hierarchy of sergeants, inspectors and superintendents. Officers were to be recruited, as far as possible, from the ranks. In overall command, and responsible to the Secretary of State, were two Commissioners. The first was Colonel Charles Rowan, an Ulsterman who had recently been a magistrate in Ireland and who was a Peninsular and Waterloo veteran: such a military record was of the greatest importance to public opinion in general. The second Commissioner was Richard Mayne, a young lawyer. While at the time of their appointment both men were unknown as public figures, they proved to be effective and efficient. The Metropolitan Police area was about 14–15 miles in diameter and covered some 1.5 million people. There were 17 divisions, designated by letters of the alphabet, with a special A Division at Whitehall to be used as a reserve establishment, whose Superintendent was senior to all others of his rank. Constables wore a blue tail-coat with metal buttons, winter trousers of the same cloth, and a heavy top-hat. They began work on 29 September 1829. In their first two years over 8,000 recruits were enrolled, of whom 4,000 resigned or were dismissed.

The hostility towards the new police was bitter and widespread, and it came from most parts of London society. The brutality against the early constables on their beats was quite extraordinary, and often encouraged by men of property. Two-thirds of the men on duty in any 24 hours were on the beat by night from 9 pm until 6 o'clock next morning; and the success of the police in diminishing burglaries, robberies and other forms of theft was quite quickly established. What was of greater political significance, however, was the increasing confrontation between the police and political demonstrators. The new Metropolitan Police had come into existence on the eve of the great Reform agitation and between the years 1830 and 1833 a series of battles were fought on the streets of London between the Radical masses and the police, during which the police established their superiority in controlling large crowds and demonstrations. Experience was learned the hard way. By the end of 1832, by which time there had been violent demonstrations and widespread damage in towns such as Nottingham and Bristol, the police in London could not yet be said to have mastered completely the tactics required for mass riot control, but it was already being remarked upon that London had not suffered the destruction that had occurred elsewhere. One important landmark in the history of riot control was the famous demonstration at Coldbath Field on 13 May 1833, when two policemen were fatally stabbed but the police finally exercised complete authority on the ground. At the inquest into the death of one of the policemen, the jury returned a verdict of 'justifiable homicide'.

The heightened political background to mass demonstrations which had been increasingly in evidence from 1815 onwards and which was to make its greatest impact during the Chartist years was responsible for the inclusion of the police clause in the 1835 Municipal Corporations Act. The significance of this Act was discussed in Chapter 4, but let it be noted here that all towns that were incorporated under the Act were required to establish a Watch Committee whose responsibility it was to appoint a professional police force for the borough. This was therefore a local system of control, with the obligation only to send to the Home Secretary a quarterly report of the numbers and equipment of the men, and any copy of the rules made by the Watch Committee or the borough council for the regulation and guidance of the officers and men. Not all the boroughs adhered to these instructions, and even when a police force was established under a Watch Committee the very common desire to keep local rates as low as possible meant that the ratio of constables to population was often well below the numerical strength that was required in the event of a serious outbreak. The Rural Police Act of 1839 extended the powers to establish police forces to the county boroughs. The magistrates at Quarter Sessions would settle the size of the force and appoint (or dismiss) the Chief Constable. The Act, however, was permissive and the obligation upon county authorities to establish police forces was not made until 1856.

While the 1835 Act was not as all-embracing for the incorporated boroughs as its sponsors wished, by the 1840s all the large towns, with only a few exceptions, had police forces which, except at times of extreme urgency, were able to cope satisfactorily with disturbances and rioting in their own areas. There were to be periods of serious crisis when the military was called in to support the civil power, but police outside London rapidly gained competence in their methods of crowd control, although the Metropolitan Police always believed in their own superiority. Within a decade of their incorporation, the largest towns all had professional forces numbering hundreds, and the coordination between the various arms of the security forces was to improve markedly as a result of the turbulent years of the Chartist period.

The professional police force could always expect some support from the special constables who would be sworn in when the local magistrates decided that they might be needed. During the first half of the nineteenth century these constables were drawn from the shopkeeping classes upwards in the social scale. Working-class enrolment as special constables was limited, at most times non-existent, but this is a matter for further research. There was certainly some participation by the labouring classes – Protestants might be enrolled in a town of many Irish Roman Catholics, with Liverpool in England as the obvious example; and in the 1840s, and especially in 1848, certain of the large public utilities, whose internal discipline was often close to approaching that of the military, compulsorily enrolled groups of their labourers. This was true in 1848 of the railway companies and the gas undertakings. There was an interesting development during the Chartist years – and it was an important marker in the ways in which working-class social consciousness was moving – when workers *inside* factories and workplaces expressed their agreement to enrol as special constables only for the purposes of defending their own places of work. This was contrary to the obligations special constables theoretically accepted when they were sworn in – which included their physical presence at places ordered by higher authority – but in the crisis conditions of certain periods of the Chartist years some support was considered to be better than none.

There was always a measure of reluctance to be enrolled as special constables, in London and elsewhere. These constables were never armed, in spite of innumerable occasions when the demand was made to the Home Office; and offered only the policeman's truncheon, many flinched from the opportunity to defend social peace and individual property. Only when the regular police had improved their own methods of crowd control and had developed a close coordination with the military – something that was noticeably improved during the 1840s – did the middle classes respond to the call for enrolment with much greater readiness. It was in 1848 that in most towns and regions the special constables became an important part of the national system of internal security.

Governments in the first half of the nineteenth century never forgot Peterloo and the unfortunate political consequences of making martyrs; it was this understanding that inhibited the use of another arm of the coercive forces at the disposal of the central authority.

The Yeomanry had been in existence since the 1790s. It was a volunteer force, made up in most counties of better-off farmers and lesser gentry. They had a standard six-day training each year and were inspected annually by a field officer of the regular army. On active service they were under military discipline, but they were controlled by the civil authorities. They could be called out by the Lord Lieutenant or by the local magistracy, but as always the Home Secretary could override any local orders and could, if necessary, devolve the control of the Yeomanry to the commanders of the various military districts. The Yeomanry were unpopular, and Whig governments in particular were reluctant to use it since they recognised that the Yeomanry's presence might often worsen a given situation. But this reluctance was never pushed too far; and when the situation in any one region or town looked menacing, and the local security forces appeared weak, then the Yeomanry would be called out. This happened in several of the Chartist years.

There was a further group at the disposal of the central government. Army pensioners had long been used as special constables and in 1843, largely in response to the massive unrest of the previous year, the government introduced a new auxiliary force: the Enrolled Pensioners. This force was composed of retired soldiers up to the age of 55, who were given eight days' training each year. When called out on active service they were armed with muskets and bayonets. Under their warrant they could be called out for 14 days in any one year; after that it was a matter of volunteering, but since they were well paid by the standard of the time there was never, it would seem, any shortage of willing recruits for duty. Their control was, as always, vested in the Home Secretary, who could mandate the Lords Lieutenant or the local military commanders as well as the mayors of the towns incorporated under the Act of 1835. The Enrolled Pensioners were a most useful reinforcement to the armed security forces. Their numbers were not large – a matter of hundreds only in the largest towns – but they were easily assembled and were trained in military discipline.

The second quarter of the nineteenth century witnessed a qualitative improvement in the organisation of the coercive powers of the British state against those of its working people who were themselves combining into effective mass movements. The growth of manufacturing and commercial activities, against the background of a rapidly increasing population, had created conditions which made urgent a major improvement in normal policing to combat rising levels of violence against property and the person. With the growth of Radical ideas and their translation into political movements, the argumented policing forces were now increasingly used against turbulence from below. It was during the Chartist years, and especially in 1848, that the enhanced efficiency of the power of the state confronted the mass movements of working people on a scale never experienced during the previous century. The year 1848 was when the central issues, of law and order in the interests of the propertied classes, were conclusively resolved.

CHAPTER 6

1848

Social unrest and popular discontent are not welcomed by the owners of capital and land in an advanced capitalist society such as Britain was becoming in the 1840s. The flow of profits and therefore of capital accumulation is slowed down or interrupted, and if the discontent begins to take physical forms – matters such as the burning down of property, the maiming of livestock or the occupation of factories or workshops – then the coercive powers of the state must be involved to restore discipline and ensure social peace. There are, of course, many ways of handling discontent. Timely reform, or its promise, can often mend broken social fences, and Corn Law repeal in 1846 and the Ten Hours Factory Bill in 1847 were examples which undoubtedly helped to persuade some groups of workers against moving forward into physical confrontation. But the sense of alienation from their own society had been growing within the consciousness of generations of working people – manifesting itself from the 1790s onwards in overt political forms – and the mass movement of Chartism was the greatest challenge the British state faced throughout the whole of the last two centuries.

The Radicalism of the first half of the nineteenth century went back, through Thomas Paine, to the American War of Independence; but the effective starting point was 1789. The 'Liberty, Equality and Fraternity' of the French revolutionaries were translated into the idiom of British Radicalism, with Tom Paine above all others as their first interpreter. France and French events were to remain a long-term influence upon British radicals, and only the French Commune of 1871 failed to evoke a response of a significant kind: a mark of the general debilitation of Radical thinking after the defeats of 1848. *The Rights of Man* began the stream of Radical ideas that steadily broadened its flow through the minds of artisans and labourers. Robert Owen began his Radical-socialist writing from 1813, and during the 1820s we see the emergence of a popular, anti-capitalist political economy developed by Thomas Hodgkin, William Thompson and John Gray. The last two had strong affinities with Robert Owen and they went well beyond the discussion of Old Corruption which Cobbett so much emphasised, although we must never play down the vigorous contribution to popular Radicalism that Cobbett himself made. The ideas of the socialists and anti-capitalists of the 1820s were popularised in widely circulated journals such as the *Poor Man's Guardian* and the *Pioneer* in the 1830s, and by writers such as Bronterre O'Brien, Henry Hetherington and James Morrison. Much of the anti-capitalist sentiment which permeated working-class speechmaking and writing, including the argument that labour is the source of all wealth, came from these and other journals.

Chartism was the word made flesh: the Radical words of the half century following Tom Paine were gradually moulded into an organised political movement on a national scale. Chartism had what all national movements of protest must have: a charismatic leadership, a Radical crusading press, the *Northern Star*, and a lively organisation at the grass roots. It was a political umbrella beneath which there gathered a number of separate protest movements, united by the Six Points of the Charter. During the best of his years Feargus O'Connor displayed all the qualities demanded of a national leader. He was a superb platform speaker with a splendid presence; wonderfully racy and vivid in his language, he could be wildly funny, both in his writings and on the platform. Above all, for much of his career he possessed the quality of self-confidence that has been so strikingly absent in most leaders of the working-class movement down to our own day. He mocked the upper classes, and denounced in blistering terms the parasites and exploiters of the ordinary people; there is no doubt of the affection and respect that he won from so many in the Radical movement during his lifetime.

The emphasis in the Six Points upon the reform of Parliament requires an explanation. In *The Condition of the Working Class in England in 1844* Friedrich Engels commented that the political objectives of the Chartist demands:

> which are all limited to the reconstruction of the House of Commons, harmless as they seem, are sufficient to overthrow the whole English Constitution, Queen and Lords included ... The English Chartist is politically a republican, though he rarely or never mentions the word, while he sympathises with the republican parties of all countries and calls himself in preference a democrat. But he is more than a mere republican, his democracy is not simply political.

The key words in this passage are democrat and democracy. Before 1848 democracy had subversive meanings. When the propertied classes referred to the mass of the people – those whom Edmund Burke had characterised as 'the swinish multitude' – it was often as 'the Democracy', with Levelling and Jacobinism as the accompanying attributes.

'The Republic of America ... is a beacon of freedom for all mankind': these were the words of a Radical journal in the early 1830s. American democracy had always been suspect to the propertied classes in England, not least because of Tom Paine's constant references to American freedom. For Robert Peel, speaking to a Glasgow audience in 1837, American governmental structures were in stark opposition to the ideas and institutions of British society. For radicals it was the absence of an Established Church and an aristocratic landlord class, the opportunities for one's own freehold, that made American life attractive. The combination of the American appeal and sympathy for French ideas was confirmation of the dangers of enfranchising the working people. Civilisation, so the historian Macaulay argued, rested on the security of property, and to give the vote to those without a property stake in the country would be to invite appropriation and confiscation. The speech which included these sentiments was made in the House of Commons debate on the second national petition of the Chartists in May 1842.

Chartism had three peaks of activity during its decade of history: in 1839–40, which included the Newport Rising in south Wales; the mass agitation around the great strike movement of 1842; and in 1848, when Europe was ablaze. All three periods were met with mass arrests, imprisonment and transportation; and with the coercive forces of the state growing steadily more powerful and more effective, in the final crisis of 1848 Chartism was annihilated. It was never to recover, and a new period of working-class history began.

The year 1848 opened on a rather dull political note. That was in England. The catastrophic famine in Ireland continued, but Ireland for the English was a country of outrages and lawlessness and mostly not for reading about in English newspapers. The previous year had seen something of a downturn in the British economy, with a financial crisis in the autumn, but most industrial and commercial sectors, except for textiles, were doing reasonably well. The event which was to dominate European affairs in 1848, and make the year a landmark in the history of many countries, was the February revolution in Paris which led quickly to the demise of the July monarchy. The happenings in France went straight on to the front pages of all the newspapers in mainland Britain, and stayed there. Naturally the response of the Radical working-class movement was one of elation and enthusiasm. In the immediate aftermath of the Paris revolution an Address to the people of Paris was adopted by the executive committee of the National Charter Association, the Fraternal Democrats and the Metropolitan Delegates Committee. The three delegates elected to take this

Address to Paris were given a boisterous send-off at a large public
meeting in London.

A France in revolutionary turmoil, with the monarchy overturned
and a provisional government already in power, inevitably evoked
among the propertied classes all over Europe the terrible images
of the Jacobin past. The reaction in Ireland was a great surge of
hope at what was happening in Paris, a fact that was immediately
taken note of by Dublin Castle and in Whitehall. In a letter of 1
March Lord John Russell, the Prime Minister, expressed the fear
that 'some attempt may be made in Dublin to emulate the barricades
of Paris ... The Irish are not the French but they have a great knack
of imitation.' For the next six months France was to occupy a central
part in the political consciousness of the whole of Britain, including
Ireland. The first manifestation of the French spirit appeared to
occur on Monday 6 March, when serious rioting broke out in
London and Glasgow. In Glasgow most of the rioters were
unemployed and there was considerable looting. The cavalry,
infantry and Enrolled Pensioners were called out and in the shooting
which followed the reading of the Riot Act a largish number of
casualties included one dead at the scene and two who later died
from their wounds.

This first indication of trouble was taken seriously by the British
authorities, not least because the news from Europe was of a
general escalation of revolutionary turmoil. There were continued
large-scale Chartist demonstrations in London and the big provincial
cities, and this allowed the security forces a constant rehearsal of
their tactics. The demonstrations also steadily increased the apprehension of the middle and upper classes, and the situation throughout
March began to harden the class alignments on the British mainland.
Corn Law repeal and its accompanying agitation were over; the
Factory Act of 1847 had roused the textile manufacturers to protest,
and there had been a flurry of opposition at the beginning of 1848
over a proposed increase in the income tax. But the fear of the revolutionary contagion passing over the Channel swept all other
considerations aside, and from the earliest days of the excitement
begun by the Paris events the solidarity of the middle classes in all
its groupings was never seriously in doubt. Palmerston, the Foreign
Secretary, wrote to the British Ambassador in Paris as early as 14
March, explaining the government's recognition of the support it
knew could be relied on:

> But the general temper of the lower and middle classes in all
> places where these riots have taken place has been excellent,
> and the best disposition has been shown by the great mass of
> the inhabitants of those places to assist the magistrates in main-
> taining order in London, and Glasgow and Edinburgh.

For the rest of March anxieties and fears increased. At a meeting in London on 13 March – attended by 4,000 police and a very much larger number of special constables – Ernest Jones announced that the London Chartists would accompany the third Chartist petition, currently being circulated, with a procession of 200,000; and for the remainder of March all meetings in London and throughout the country had large security forces in attendance. The announcement that a national Chartist Convention would meet in London before the presentation of the third petition greatly encouraged the hysteria that was enveloping the country in a quite remarkable fashion.

The Convention, which opened on 4 April, was limited to 49 delegates from round the country: a limitation imposed by the law against assemblies of larger numbers. A number of fiery speeches were made extolling the example of the Parisian workers, and there were speeches of moderation, but the mood of public opinion was such that inevitably it was the language of physical force that received the greatest publicity. Few periods in the past two centuries can compare with the panic which seized large numbers of the British people, especially those in London where the demonstration of 10 April was to precede the march to Westminster in order to present the national petition. Many really did believe that the revolutionary events in Paris would be repeated in London.

The control of the security forces was the responsibility of the Home Secretary, Sir George Grey, an effective parliamentarian and an excellent administrator. Grey was never in doubt that the situation could be contained. He and his colleagues were responsible for the whole of the United Kingdom, including the disposition of the military forces. There were two Under-Secretaries of State at the Home Office, including one Parliamentary Under-Secretary who normally dealt with parliamentary matters, Ireland, Scotland and the Channel Islands. Since Ireland had a separate administration in Dublin, there was close liaison between the Parliamentary Under-Secretary and the Irish Chief Secretary, who always remained in London during parliamentary sessions. The second Permanent Under-Secretary, a civil servant, was always a barrister and dealt with legal questions in general. Working with the Home Secretary and his two senior colleagues was a small bureaucracy of civil servants, about half a dozen of whom had important administrative responsibilities. Altogether in 1848, excluding manual workers, there were no more than 22 civil servants in the Home Office staff, about double the number of half a century earlier. Assisting the Home Secretary were the law officers of the Crown and the Military Secretary at the War Office (usually referred to as the Horse Guards). The Duke of Wellington as Commander-in-Chief has usually been credited with responsibility for the disposition of troops on 10 April, but he was in fact largely by-passed during these days by the Military Secretary, Lieutenant-General Sir Fitzroy Somerset, who maintained very close contact with the Home Office.

The Queen and her family left London for the Isle of Wight on the morning of 8 April, and in these last few days before the 10th the authorities in London set about making their dispositions. All public buildings were heavily guarded in order to prevent the establishment of bases for the 'revolutionaries', as had happened in Paris. The total number of troops was 7,122, including cavalry, and they were dispersed out of sight. There were just over 4,000 police, 1,231 Enrolled Pensioners and about 85,000 special constables. The distinguishing feature of the measures taken by the British government was the overwhelming support they generated from the middle strata all over the country, and certainly in London. The firmness and competence of the Home Office direction of affairs helped a great deal, for the 'specials' could now feel wholly confident of both police and military support.

For the Whig government the meeting on Kennington Common on 10 April was of quite major importance. The Chartist demonstration was never intended to be a physical confrontation with the government; although some of the inflammatory speeches before the 10th had been picked upon by the press and widely discussed, when the majority of the Chartist leaders protested their peaceful intentions they were not dissembling. It was not, however, just London that was becoming more and more anxious as to the outcome of the meeting. Throughout Britain and Ireland, and also in the main cities in Europe and above all Paris, the Kennington Common demonstration was being looked upon as an event whose outcome might have incalculable consequences for the revolutionary movement of the future. But it was not hysteria that moved the Whig ministers to devise such elaborate precautions. They were certainly not going to permit the procession to Westminster as an accompaniment to the national petition; but to contain the Chartist demonstration with their own demonstration of strength was enormously worthwhile. And this is what happened. The Kennington Common meeting was a failure. The Chartists were trapped south of the river with all the bridges over the Thames too heavily guarded for any movement across them; and among the Chartist leadership, after an agreement to abandon the procession to the Houses of Parliament, there was inevitably a sense of anticlimax once the speeches were over. The news of the government 'victory' was telegraphed round the country and in the large towns the local corporations placarded their towns with the information; in Dublin and Paris it was received with dismay.

Yet the government, unlike many later historians, was under no illusions that the agitation in the country as a whole was at an end. The failure of 10 April in London had a somewhat dampening effect for a few weeks, but elsewhere it seemed to have little or no impact. Throughout the summer of 1848 the areas most affected by disturbance and riot were the industrial towns of the West Riding and Lancashire, and the metropolitan centre of London. The presence of Irish immigrants was nearly always a factor making for more violent physical confrontation along with the native-born English or Scots; and events in Ireland were followed with enthusiastic support. In the towns and regions mentioned the levels of agitation and demonstrations of physical force continued to rise during the late spring and through the summer months until August. In London the continuous marchings and processions began to concern upper-class opinion and the public prints, and calls were made for definitive action. On 6 June warrants were issued for the arrest of Ernest Jones, the most important leader in London, and other prominent Chartists. The week which followed was similar to the events preceding Kennington Common. The appeal of the executive committee of the National Charter Association for a mass meeting on Monday 12 June – which happened to be Whit Monday – was met with a ban on all demonstrations in London, and the security preparations were equal to those for 10 April. Guns and artillerymen were brought from Woolwich, all major public buildings were heavily guarded and the meeting place of Bonner's Fields was occupied by large bodies of police.

In the industrial north, Bradford was probably the town with the most potentially dangerous situation, although Manchester and Liverpool, as well as some of the smaller textile towns, continued throughout these months to present constant problems for the security forces. One of the most interesting developments in this very troubled year was the rapport which came about between the military commanders and the businessmen who were mayors of the large towns. Manchester provides a good example. The military commander for the Northern Command – the largest of the military districts – was Lieutenant-General Sir Thomas Arbuthnot, a Peninsular veteran and a man of considerable ability and shrewdness. His letters to the Home Office make very informative reading. The Lord Mayor of Manchester was Elkanah Armitage, and he and his fellow magistrates were mainly Liberal Dissenters, anti-aristocratic as middle-class merchants and manufacturers usually were, and often with an anti-militarist tradition. What brought the civil and military authorities together in close working harmony was their common opposition to the harsh verbal attacks on property and privilege and the resort to riot and violence. Armitage himself was born in 1794, so he was considerably younger than General Arbuthnot. He had begun with a small draper's shop, from which he graduated to become a bedding manufacturer with mills at Swinton and Pendleton. He was elected Lord Mayor in November 1846 and served for two years, and at the end of his term of office the Home Secretary recommended him for a knighthood. What was especially noticeable about the Manchester situation – and it was reproduced elsewhere – was the steady shift towards a hardline position as the months of continued turbulence went by. At the beginning of the 'troubles' many middle-class public figures showed some sympathy with the demands coming from below. They too were against the Established Church and Tory/aristocratic domination of the Houses of Parliament; but by the end of the year, as a result of the continuous pressure of violent language and threatened or actual physical violence, they were not to be distinguished from aristo-cratic Whigs or Tories on all fundamental issues relating to law, order and the sanctity of property rights.

This reshaping of political alignments was to be observed around the country. Of all the towns in the textile districts Bradford, as already noted, was probably the most potentially revolutionary from the spring of 1848 to the falling away of the mass movement everywhere after the late summer. Mid-century Bradford epitomised the technology as well as the class relations of the developing industry state. Weaving was almost completely mechanised in the worsted trade by 1848, although quite a number of firms continued to operate with a mixed system of hand and factory workers. The mechanisation of woolcombing had been much more drawn out and the hand woolcombers, numbering some 10,000 workers, were now among the most exploited and miserable of all textile workers. Housing conditions were appalling and wages were low and irregular. Again the propertied middle class had a number of reforming aims in common with the Bradford Chartists, but the continuous conflict throughout the year hardened attitudes and drew sharp political lines where previously there had been some overlap of attitudes. The mayor, Robert Milligan, was a self-made merchant, liberal-Radical in politics and a Nonconformist in religion.

One of the critical days of this turbulent summer in Bradford was Monday 29 May. An attempt to arrest two local Chartist leaders early in the morning by several hundred special constables, with only a few of the professional police in support, had failed after a ferocious fight, and after their victory working-class groups began to move into the centre of the town. Shops were shut and tensions increased. It was clearly necessary for the security forces to regain control. All special constables were ordered to be in position by 3.30 of the same afternoon. The Halifax Yeomanry was held in reserve – the Bradford troop had been sent to Huddersfield. At 4 pm the whole of the professional police, armed with cutlasses, marched from the centre of the town followed by 1,000 special constables with their staves or truncheons, together with the mayor and all the magistrates. At their back were 200 infantry with fixed bayonets, with two troops of dragoons bringing up the rear. Alongside the mayor marched Joshua Pollard, one of the largest landowners in the district, coalmine owner, manager of an ironworks and a Tory in politics: this was once more a closing of the ranks of the propertied against the threats from below. On this occasion there was again fierce resistance at the place of fighting in the morning and only the use of the cavalry salvaged the position for the authorities.

Throughout these middle months of 1848 the general situation in Ireland continued to deteriorate. The arrest of John Mitchel, Smith O'Brien and T.F. Meagher in late March had increased the tension. O'Brien and Meagher were brought to trial in mid-May but due to the presence of at least one Catholic on the jury they could not be convicted. When Mitchel was brought to trial the Irish administration made certain of the result. Mitchel was charged under the new Crown and Security Act, passed the previous April and commonly known as the Treason-Felony Act; the jury was packed, with no Catholic in its numbers; and Mitchel was sentenced to 14 years' transportation. He was quickly hurried out of the country.

His trial had already led to demonstrations in the areas of England where there were large numbers of Catholics, and his conviction helped to bring the Irish and the Chartists closer together. There is still legitimate argument concerning the relationship between English Radicals and the immigrant Irish during the 1830s and 1840s, but there is no question of the growing bond between them during 1848: a coming together of which both Dublin Castle and Whitehall were fully conscious. It could have been closer and more integrated. The worsening situation in Ireland led the Home Office to introduce the suspension of Habeas Corpus in Ireland on 25 July and rumours of a coming insurrection continued to circulate in Britain, and again notably in the towns where the Irish population was large. Liverpool was the most affected, and security arrangements there were steadily expanded. The strength of the police force was increased by 500, and a tented encampment for the military was established at Everton. Gunboats went up and down the Mersey. The most remarkable exhibition of the panic which by now had seized the middle classes of Liverpool was a petition opened on the day that the suspension of Habeas Corpus was introduced in the House of Commons, to the effect that the Bill should be extended to the city of Liverpool. It was signed by the mayor and all the Liverpool magistrates save one. By the time it was presented to the House of Commons on 25 July, it had around 1,000 signatures, including some of the best-known names of the liberal community.

The Radical movements on both sides of the Irish Sea reached their high points during July and August 1848 at the same time as the Westminster government and Dublin Castle began arresting and imprisoning the greater part of the leaderships in both Britain and Ireland. It is not certain whether there was a serious illegal movement linking London with some of the northern centres, but by mid-August the most important leaders of Chartism, both at the national and at the local and regional level, had been arrested. The Chartist National Assembly in May had appointed an executive committee of five: the most active were Ernest Jones and Peter McDougall, both of whom were arrested and imprisoned for two years. Feargus O'Connor at this time was almost completely occupied with the official enquiry into the Land Plan and in any case was quite out of sympathy with the militant trends in the movement, while the other two members were not personalities of national stature. The Assembly had also elected 20 commission- ers, of whom at least 14 can be identified as having been arrested and convicted between May and September. By the end of August several hundreds of Chartists and Irish Confederates had been arrested in London and the northern industrial towns. The government had overwhelmed the movement by physical force. In Manchester, for example, the final arrests began in the evening of Tuesday 15 August and continued for the next week. The police and military backing for these arrests was formidable: 300 armed police (with cutlasses), two companies of the 30th Foot and two troops of the Royal Irish Dragoons.

In Ireland it was Mitchel's conviction that began the last phase of open conspiracy and insurgency, and the language of defiance became ever more violent. Throughout June and July arrests continued and the attempted 'rebellion' of early August – a miserably planned affair – was quickly brought under control, marking the end of any effective movement of opposition.

The great and outstanding merit of English law, in periods when the propertied classes have found themselves or thought they have found themselves threatened, has been its extraordinary flexibil- ity. For the nineteenth century, A.V. Dicey's *Law of the Constitution* summed up what his contemporaries believed to be a correct inter- pretation; although Dicey has been much criticised by modern scholars, his sections on the right to freedom of speech and the right of public meeting are highly relevant to the present analysis. 'At no time has there been in England any proclamation of the right to liberty of thought or freedom of speech', Dicey wrote, and similarly the right of public meeting was never recognised as a specific or basic right of the citizen. What was critical in the matter of freedom of speech, Dicey argued, was the condition of 'popular sentiment' as interpreted both by the presiding judges and the representatives of the jury-serving classes. No year in the nineteenth century illustrated more strikingly the varying interpretation of liberty of expression than 1848 in England. There was always what Holdsworth called the 'usual attitude of deference' of the juries to their judges, and in 1848, by the time most trials of Chartists and Irish Radicals were held, there was added the solid conviction among the jury-serving classes that Chartism and related manifestations of discontent from below must be put down and thoroughly crushed. The Irish legal system had its own quirks and differences, but the general outcome was the same.

The Home Office, from March until the end of May, had pursued a fairly consistent policy of refusing requests from local magistrates for the arrest of Chartist speakers. The cautiousness of Whitehall was based upon the recognition that prosecutions which failed to win convictions would damage their general strategy for law and order. There was still some uncertainty about the wholeheartedness of sections of the middle classes in the matter of aligning themselves with the Whig aristocracy and Tory reaction. It was the continuing surge of discontent coming from the ordinary people and the recognition of middle-class alarm at what was happening that altered Whitehall's appreciation of the shifts in public, that is middle-class, opinion. There were enough legal statutes under which the judiciary could be expected to do their duty to the state, and the only new legislation of importance was the Crown and Security Act of April 1848, the so-called Treason-Felony Act. Hitherto successful prosecutions for treason had been followed by death; the new Act kept the old penalties for direct offences against the sovereign, but for the rest, treasons were felonies, no longer punishable by death but by transportation for not less than seven years, or by imprisonment for two years, with or without hard labour. A new clause would now allow prosecution for 'open and advised speaking'. Altogether this was a useful umbrella Act which permitted much wider licence to both prosecution counsels and presiding judges.

The legal assault upon the Chartist movement in London came with the arrest in early June of Ernest Jones, now the most important leader in the country as a whole, and as already noted the next three months saw many hundreds taken into custody. Eight judges belonging to one or other of the three common law courts sat on most political cases this year, either at the Central Criminal Court in London or at the Assizes in the provinces. There were inevitably differences in the range and depth of their learning, but what is remarkable is that they all talked exactly the same language in respect of the political prisoners before them. Differences between Whig and Tory were not to be discerned; the prejudices of their upper class contemporaries were their prejudices; with the middle classes of England they had glimpsed the red dawn on European horizons, and they contemplated with horror the abyss opening beneath them. Their language was the language of the learned, their ideas were grammatical versions of the comfortable self-made grocer. To their juries they explained the virtues of English liberty and the wickedness of the prisoners in the dock, or at best their naive illusions; and they left no one in doubt as to the guilt of the accused. These English political trials of 1848 were grotesque exercises in the miscarriage of justice; prejudice overcame reason and legal principles were submerged beneath partiality of a malevolent order.

By a curious twist of history there were two political trials in Scotland in this year that exhibited a legal probity wholly missing in the courts of England. During the 1790s Scottish trials had been a brutal travesty of the law, but in 1848, while the indictments were very similar to those of the English political prisoners, the trials were conducted with a recognition of the decencies to be accorded to the prisoners in the dock, and this was observed by the prosecuting counsels as well as by the judges in their directions to the juries.

Ireland, as would be expected, followed even more crudely the English pattern. The most important political trial after that of John Mitchel was the indictment for high treason of Smith O'Brien following the abortive attempt at a rising in late July and early August. All three judges were Protestant; the jury was rigged, and there were a number of other irregularities against which the defending counsels protested. The defence team was first class, much superior to the defence lawyers who acted for the Chartist prisoners in England. But this was to no avail. Government and police informers had been a common feature of the English trials and so they were in Ireland. The chief informer in the Smith O'Brien trial was taken apart in devastating fashion by the leading defence lawyer, but it made no difference to the Lord Chief Justice or his colleagues. The defence entered an appeal, first in Dublin and then, when that was turned down, in the House of Lords, where the man who delivered the judgement against the appeal was none other than the senior judge in the English political trials.

Epilogue

The mass discontent and its Radical political expression in a nationwide political movement quickly faded after 1848. In the 1840s the economic depression of the years up to 1842 had been exceptionally severe, but it was succeeded by a high level of investment, a boom in railway building, banking and commercial reforms, all of which contributed to a vigorous upward movement of the economy. The second half of 1847 saw a quite serious economic crisis, with unemployment on a large scale in the last quarter of the year and for the first half of 1848, but had it not been for the European revolutions the return to upward growth would not have had to wait until the last months of 1848. The secular expansion of the British economy as a whole reached its highest levels for the whole century between the 1840s and the 1870s. The course of business and commercial activity ran more smoothly in the third quarter than earlier, and employment generally improved – without ever, of course, approaching full employment except in occasional years.

It was not only the greater regularity of work, or rising living standards, especially for the skilled workers, that brought about the very marked change in political attitudes among working people during the third quarter of the nineteenth century. These were without doubt important contributory factors, but there is no simple causative analysis that can be offered for the historic fracture in working-class political consciousness which followed 1848. The roots of reformism of the kind that came to dominate the middle decades after 1848 can be uncovered before the mid-century. There was always a notable constitutional strain within important groups of working-class activists. The influence of the various sects of Nonconformity tended to encourage quietism in political terms, or a non-violent approach; and the influence of religion upon many groups and occupations must never be underestimated. Before 1850 there was a notable growth of defensive institutions such as friendly societies or trade unions among the skilled workers, but the degree of 'defensiveness' in working-class organisations depends very much upon the context within which the various groups are operating. The foundations of the Labourist philosophy that developed after 1850 lay in the work situation, and the phrase which summed up the Labourist attitude was 'A Fair Day's Work for a Fair Day's Pay'. Its meaning for trade unionists was always more complex than has often been appreciated. There was, on the one hand, a recognition that fair dealing was available, or at least thought to be available, in capitalist society; but on the other, among the well-organised crafts, there was a stubborn insistence upon traditional bargaining rights at the point of production. Moreover, in the years after 1850 there were claims for trade unions which came to be regarded as being of crucial importance. Any threat, for example, to the legal status of trade unions would call forth considerable reserves of intransigence and class opposition. It was never easy, for trade unionism became a bogey for middle-class opinion that has remained central to its thinking on industrial affairs up to the present time; and after 1850 it took a further quarter of a century before substantial changes in the law relating to trade unions appeared on the statute book.

What has usually been missed in the analysis of historical change around the middle of the nineteenth century has been the physical destruction of the mass movement of working people by the now greatly enhanced efficiency of the coercive power of the British state. The mass imprisonment, transportation and successful confrontation of the mass demonstrations during the three main periods of the Chartist years – 1839–40, 1842 and 1848 – contributed significantly to the disintegration of the national movement. Without that physical assault upon the militant sections of the Chartist leadership and of so many of the second-line activists, the aftermath in the 1850s might have been different. It might also have been different had the ideas of 'The Charter and Something More' which Ernest Jones was enunciating after his two years' imprisonment become part of political consciousness in the years before 1848.

The effective consolidation of the British state by the third quarter of the nineteenth century was a product of a rapidly developing industrial society, of a middle class whose ideology of laissez-faire and the free market was a central article of faith linked with an unshakeable belief in a confident future. The political reforms of the 1830s and 1840s brought the traditional ruling class and the owners of capital into a political accommodation which above all recognised the need for unity against the threats to the rights of property. A turbulent and dissatisfied working people was not helpful, and although their activities could be contained by oppressive laws and improved policing, it was their political attitudes that had finally to be confronted, and defeated. That was the meaning of 1848, and for the rich and the powerful, and their middle-class allies, it was a famous victory.

The working-class presence in British society after the 1840s could not, however, be ignored. It had been restricted and constrained, and its ultra-radical politics submerged, but intelligent members of the propertied classes recognised the need for degrees of consent. Factory reform and working-class education had their meagre beginnings before 1850, and social reform began slowly – very slowly – to be extended. It was matched on the side of government by the beginnings of civil service reform in the mid-1850s, structured in ways that made certain the gentlemen of England would continue to occupy all the top administrative positions. Radical reform always had to be vigorously fought for, and by the time it was achieved most of the radical content had been removed. Britain after 1850 remained a deeply conservative society, and for the rest of the century social and political change was halting, limited and incomplete.

Gladstone, later to be titled 'The People's William', should have the last word. He had been warned during the year 1865 that the liberal approach to a number of political issues, particularly the extension of the franchise, was causing alarm and opposition among the propertied classes, especially of the traditional kind. Gladstone replied (although his 'goodwill' should not be taken too literally):

> Please to recollect that we have to govern millions of hard hands; that it must be done by force, fraud or goodwill; that the latter has been tried and is answering; that none have profited more by this change of system since the corn law and the six Acts, than those who complain of it.

Additional Reading

The starting point for a socialist understanding of capitalist society must be Karl Marx's own writings. For the present work the last section of Volume 1 of *Capital*, 'The So-called Primitive Accumulation' is the necessary introduction. The classic work by Friedrich Engels, *The Condition of the Working Class in England*, should also be necessary reading. The first German edition was published in 1845; the first English in 1892. There are many editions, including a paperback by Panther Books (London, 1969) with a most helpful introduction by Eric Hobsbawm. *A Dictionary of Marxist Thought*, edited by Tom Bottomore (Blackwell, Oxford, 1983) will be found useful; see especially the entries on Capitalism; Forces and Relations of Production; Law; Ruling Class; the State; Working Class; Working Class Movements. Each entry has bibliographies attached. For a good general text, see E.J. Hobsbawm, *Industry and Empire: An Economic History of Britain since 1750* (Weidenfeld and Nicolson, London, 1968; various paperback editions). There were two general histories of an older generation that were widely read: A.L. Morton, *A People's History of England* (Gollancz, London, 1938) and G.D.H. Cole and R. Postgate, *The Common People, 1746–1946* (2nd edn. Methuen, London, 1946).

For a much more detailed account of early industrialisation in Britain, there is an excellent text by S. Pollard, *The Genesis of Modern Management: a Study of the Industrial Revolution in Great Britain* (Penguin, Harmondsworth, 1968); further material will be found in Maxine Berg, *The Age of Manufactures: Industry, Innovation and Work in Britain, 1700–1820* (Blackwell, Oxford, 1985). Eighteenth-century economic and political history has been enriched with the publication by John Brewer of *The Sinews of Power: War, Money and the English State, 1688–1783* (Unwin Hyman, London, 1989).

Two books by John Rule provide a close appreciation of the working classes in early industrialisation: *The Experience of Labour in Eighteenth-Century Industry* (Croom Helm, London, 1981) and *The Labouring Classes in Early Industrial England* (Longman, Harlow, 1986). For the same period, J.L. and Barbara Hammond wrote three classic texts: *The Village Labourer, Town Labourer* and *The Skilled Labourer* (Various editions, mostly 1911–1927).

The most important study of working-class Radicalism and one of the great historical texts of the twentieth century is Edward Thompson, *The Making of the English Working Class* (Gollancz, London, 1963; paperback edn. with new postscript, Penguin, Harmondsworth, 1968). The beginnings of working-class Radicalism are described in two booklets published by the Historical Association: H.T. Dickinson, *British Radicalism and the French Revolution, 1789–1815* and J.R. Dinwiddy, *From Luddism to the First Reform Bill* (both published by Blackwell, Oxford, 1985 and 1986). On the politics of 1832 there is a useful booklet by Eric J. Evans, *The Great Reform Act of 1832* (Lancaster pamphlets, Routledge, London, 1983).

There is relatively little published on the relations between the law and working people. The standard text, not especially easy reading but comprehensive, is W.R. Cornish and G. de N. Clark, *Law and Society in England, 1750–1950* (Sweet and Maxwell, London, 1989). The discussion in the present text of the Master and Servants legislation is based largely on an essay by Daphne Simon published some 40 years ago: 'Master and Servant', in *Democracy and the Labour Movement*, ed. J. Saville (Lawrence and Wishart, London, 1954), pp. 160–200. The growth of the coercive powers of the state is discussed in detail in John Saville, *1848: The British State and the Chartist Movement* (Cambridge University Press, 1987 and paperback, 1990). The major pioneering work in this field was F.C. Mather, *Public Order in the Age of the Chartists* (Manchester University Press, 1959).

Index

outworkers 15–16, 23
Owen, Robert 68
ownership
  land 49–51, 55
  means of production 2

Paine, Thomas 68, 69, 70
Palmerston, Henry 36, 51, 71
parish relief 25–8
parliament
  Irish interests after Union
    51
  power and corruption 6,
    41–3
  'Old Corruption' 41, 42,
    50, 68
  see also politics; Reform
    movement
patent law 32–3
pauper children, apprenticeship 17
Peace Preservation Force 56
Peel, Robert 52, 70
  police reform 56, 62–3
peerage 41
Pentridge revolution 61
perquisites, as part of wages
  15
Peterloo killings 45, 61, 65
Petty, Sir William 33–4
Pioneer 69
police
  before reform 54
  control of demonstrations
    44, 73, 75–6
  establishment of forces
    63–5
  and freemasons 57–8
  hostility toward 63
  Irish 56–8
  reform 56, 61–3
  special constables 58, 60,
    65, 73
politics
  alignments 71–2, 75, 76,
    78–9

corruption 41–3
  'Old Corruption' 41, 42,
    50, 68
political consciousness
  of middle class 36–7
  of working class 28, 80
  see also Chartism
reform see Reform
  movement
trials 78–9
Poor Law Commission 26–7
Poor Law policy 25–8
Poor Man's Guardian 43, 69
poor relief 25–8
population
  agricultural 2, 13
  growth 13
  and crime 54, 58
pottery industry 31
poverty vii, 14–15, 50–1, 55
  see also poor relief
power
  of aristocracy maintained
    after Reform 46–51, 53
  shared viii, 5, 46–53
  war as means of obtaining
    7–8
production, capitalist mode 2
protectionism 5

Quarterly Review 39

radicalism 43, 66–7, 68
railways 12
  and troop movement 44,
    55, 60
Reform movement 36–40,
    43–5, 63–4
  Reform Act (1832) viii, 44,
    45–6
religion
  British attitudes to Ireland
    56
  Church corruption 43, 51,
    53, 55
  clergymen as magistrates 59